Music Secrets for the Advanced Musician
A Scarecrow Press Music Series

Music Secrets for the Advanced Musician is designed for instrumentalists, singers, conductors, composers, and other instructors and professionals in music seeking a quick set of pointers to improve their work as performers and creators of music. Easy to use and intended for the advanced musician, contributions to **Music Secrets** fill a niche for those who have moved far beyond what beginners and intermediate practitioners need. It is the perfect resource for teaching students what they need to know in order to take that next step forward and for reinforcing a set of best practices among advanced and professional musicians.

Clarinet Secrets: 52 Performance Strategies for the Advanced Clarinetist, 2nd edition, by Michele Gingras, 2006

Saxophone Secrets: 60 Performance Strategies for the Advanced Saxophonist, by Tracy Lee Heavner, 2013

Oboe Secrets: 75 Performance Strategies for the Advanced Oboist and English Horn Player, by Jacqueline Leclair, 2013

Drum Kit Secrets: 52 Performance Strategies for the Advanced Drummer, by Matt Dean, 2014

Drum Kit Secrets

52 Performance Strategies for the Advanced Drummer

Matt Dean

Music Secrets for the Advanced Musician

THE SCARECROW PRESS, INC.
Lanham • Boulder • New York • Toronto • Plymouth, UK
2014

Published by Scarecrow Press, Inc.
A wholly owned subsidiary of Rowman & Littlefield
4501 Forbes Boulevard, Suite 200, Lanham, Maryland 20706
www.rowman.com

10 Thornbury Road, Plymouth PL6 7PP, United Kingdom

British Library Cataloguing in Publication Information Available

Library of Congress Cataloging-in-Publication Data
Dean, Matt, 1980–
  Drum kit secrets : 52 performance strategies for the advanced drummer / Matt Dean.
      pages cm. — (Music secrets for the advanced musician)
  Includes bibliographical references and index.
  ISBN 978-0-8108-8695-7 (pbk : alk. paper) — ISBN 978-0-8108-8696-4 (ebook) 1.
Drum set—Instruction and study. I. Title.
  MT662.D42 2014
  786.9'193—dc23   2013030029

∞™ The paper used in this publication meets the minimum requirements of
American National Standard for Information Sciences—Permanence of
Paper for Printed Library Materials, ANSI/NISO Z39.48-1992.

Printed in the United States of America.

To the daughter I never met but will never forget.
And to the wife and son that make me smile every day.

Contents

Preface   xi

Acknowledgments   xiii

1 Practice Strategies   1

Secret 1: Time Management   1

Secret 2: Practice Diary   5

Secret 3: Record Yourself   6

Secret 4: Rhythm Then Orchestration   7

Secret 5: Add a Note   8

Secret 6: Looping   10

Secret 7: Don't Forget to Breathe   12

Secret 8: Best Sticking   13

Secret 9: Avoid the Rut—How to Find Inspiration   15

Secret 10: Play More with Less   18

2 Technique Strategies   21

Secret 11: Play without Tension   21

Secret 12: The Bounce   24

Secret 13: Which Grip?   28

Secret 14: Fundamental Bass Techniques   31

Secret 15: Nature's Way   36

3 Timing Strategies   39

Secret 16: Developing Your Internal Metronome   39

Secret 17: Master of the Metronome   42

Secret 18: Find Your Achilles' Heel   44

Secret 19: Swinging   47

Secret 20: Odd Time   50

4   Accuracy Strategies   53
   Secret 21: Locked Limbs   53
   Secret 22: Speed Bursts   56

5   Equipment Strategies   59
   Secret 23: Choosing Drums   59
   Secret 24: Choosing Cymbals   63
   Secret 25: Choosing Drumsticks   65
   Secret 26: Tuning—The Black Art   67
   Secret 27: Eliminating Snare Buzz   75
   Secret 28: Getting the Right Snare Sound for Each Song   77
   Secret 29: Essential Equipment   80
   Secret 30: Embracing Technology   82

6   Health Strategies   87
   Secret 31: Protecting Your Greatest Instrument   87
   Secret 32: Looking After Your Back   91
   Secret 33: Optimizing Setup and Seat Position   97
   Secret 34: Potential Health Risks   100

7   Preparation Strategies   105
   Secret 35: Writing Charts Quickly   105
   Secret 36: Nailing the Audition   109
   Secret 37: Financial Planning   112

8   Marketability Strategies   115
   Secret 38: Learn All Styles to a Passable Level   115
   Secret 39: Focus Your Efforts   118
   Secret 40: Promoting Yourself   120
   Secret 41: Maximize Your Employability   122
   Secret 42: Keeping the Gigs—Beyond Drumming   125

9   Recording Strategies   127
   Secret 43: Play Less   127
   Secret 44: Playing for the Song   129
   Secret 45: Achieving a Great Tone   131
   Secret 46: Mix Yourself   133

10 Performance Strategies   135
   Secret 47: Warm-up and Gig Preparation   135
   Secret 48: Stage Fright   137
   Secret 49: Believe in Yourself   141

11 Soloing Strategies   143
    Secret 50: Soloing with a Theme   143
    Secret 51: Odd Numbered Groupings   147
    Secret 52: Jumping into the Abyss—Improvising   150

Bibliography   153

Index   155

About the Author   157

Preface

This book is written for the advanced drum kit player in need of specific strategies to overcome recurring technical and musical challenges. It is assumed that readers have already attained a high level of competency on the drum kit and are looking to push themselves to the highest level possible.

Some of the concepts, advice, and ideas in this book cover more basic yet essential practices, while others are much more advanced and take a deeper level of understanding of the instrument.

The hope is that this book will add to the readers' knowledge and help them build a career through their instrument and enjoy longevity by maximizing the ability to move between different areas of the music industry to maintain a living from their passion.

The material in this book has been acquired from more than twenty years of playing, fifteen years of teaching, more than ten years of professional performance, and many interviews and conversations with great musicians.

The topics covered include how to maintain your equipment, how to stay healthy, how to market yourself professionally, how to overcome stage fright, how to manage your time, how to focus your mind, how to develop accuracy, how to develop certain drumming techniques, how to use modern music technology, how to select the right equipment, how to prepare for gigs and auditions, how to work in a studio environment, how to solo, and much more.

In order to tackle each problem immediately, each strategy or "secret" is described in a concise manner, breaking the problem down and offering practical solutions. The secrets are set out in a clear and easy-to-read layout so the book can be read in whole or used as a reference for specific issues when they arise.

Many of these strategies have helped me along the way so I hope that readers will find the book a useful addition to their drumming armory.

Matt Dean
www.mattdeanworld.co.uk

Acknowledgments

The ideas within this book were already compiled long before this book was ever conceptualized. Through years of my own playing and facing musical challenges, I have had to ask questions, seek answers, find solutions, and enjoy being lucky enough to receive great advice from teachers, peers, and colleagues.

Since my becoming a teacher of the drum kit, my students have constantly asked me the same kinds of questions I once asked myself. This has forced me to consider those answers even more deeply in order to address them adequately.

Therefore, I must thank every student who has ever asked me a difficult question or caused me to consider my own approach to drum kit playing. I would also like to thank tutors who have contributed to my knowledge over the years: Mike Sturgis, Pete Riley, Bill Bruford, and Andrew Small.

I would like to thank every drummer in the world, from seasoned professional to early beginner, who offered me daily inspiration and motivation. That list would be too large for me to include.

And, of course, I must thank my family: my parents who allowed me to follow my dreams, my wife who puts up with me following my dream, and my three-year-old son who accepts only spending time with me following my dream and who will at some point realize that hitting things with bits of wood isn't a "real" job. I love you all.

CHAPTER 1

Practice Strategies

SECRET 1: TIME MANAGEMENT

Modern life is hectic; time is a valuable commodity, and most of us would like more of it. But most of us have also been guilty of procrastinating and time wasting at some point. This can greatly reduce our development as drummers if vast periods of potential practice time are squandered.

My typical week involves a combination of performances, rehearsals, recording sessions, article writing, teaching, and preparation. Much of this is scheduled with a very strict deadline, and somewhere within it I have to make sure I'm ready for each commitment, not to mention family time and other leisure activities.

If we carefully plan our time, set our goals, and see the plan through, we can optimize how that time is spent and therefore develop much more effectively as musicians. While everyone works in slightly different ways, giving your practice sessions structure will vastly improve your efficiency.

Here are some tips to help you achieve this:

1. Plan practice sessions in your diary and don't let them slip away.

Having set periods for practice in your diary means that you are much more likely to carry out those practice sessions. That is your designated time to completely focus on that task. Leave any other issues at the door and allow your body and mind to optimize that time for developing your playing.

2. Don't multitask.

We often multitask in life. Although making a cup of tea while cooking dinner and carrying out a phone conversation might be a great time-saver, trying to practice several things at once results in no single aspect being given the full focus that it needs to acquire the necessary level of performance required at a professional level. Break your practice session into sections and use each section to concentrate on a single technique, passage of music, and so on. This way you will retain the information and body movements to a greater extent.

3. Prioritize!

Practice the most important (and most difficult) exercises first. This is the time when you are freshest and most inspired and motivated. If you have a gig tomorrow, learn that material before anything else.

4. Capitalize on free time.

Downtime in the hotel while on tour, coffee breaks between teaching, the dressing room before a show—these are all moments that you can use to work on new material if you are properly equipped. Take a practice pad, manuscript paper, and sticks wherever you go and every spare moment becomes a practice session.

5. Banish distractions—Facebook, e-mails, Twitter, and so on.

Distractions are everywhere. You have instant access to texts, e-mails, social media sites, and much more via your computer, tablet, and mobile phone. And with the cheery notification ping that these devices provide, even tucked away in your bag, they still let you know when something has come through. But stop and think: do you really need to break your concentration only to find out through Facebook that Aunty Ethel has just baked an amazing apple crumble? Probably not. Turn all devices off, find an isolated space away from family and friends, close the door, and fully commit your mind and body to your practice. The rewards will be great.

6. Find your most productive time of the day and use it.

Some of us are night owls; some early birds. Try to identify when you are naturally most productive and, where possible, plan your practice sessions for then. Of course if, like me, you come alive close to midnight, drumming might not go down well with the neighbors. But where possible, use your naturally motivated moments to create greater gains in the sessions.

7. Set very clear SMART goals.

This acronym is a useful way to keep yourself on track. I am definitely prone to setting myself unrealistic targets for the time I have available. The result is either poor-quality, rushed work or achieving none of the goals because I was overwhelmed. By using the SMART system, you will have a very clear idea of what needs to be achieved and how to go about it.

S—Specific

Unambiguous goals are crucial. You might have a piece to learn for a performance next week. This goal is clear. But sitting down to practice simply to become a better drummer might leave you overwhelmed with the numerous techniques and disciplines available to a drummer. That isn't to say that just sitting at the kit and playing for pure enjoyment is a waste of time; on the contrary, this is important and great fun. But when you have time pressure for an upcoming performance, exam, or audition, make sure you set specific goals in order to be ready.

M—Measurable

The goal of "being an amazing drummer" is difficult to quantify. Being amazing is subjective. When will you know you're amazing? And besides, along the way, there will be years of disappointment when you're not amazing in your eyes. Smaller, more frequent successes will keep you highly motivated, and measurable goals make it easier to know when to give yourself a pat on the back. For example, let's say you want to play even semiquaver double strokes at 200 bpm. This goal is easy to determine once you have achieved it.

A—Attainable

It is important that you stretch yourself, but not to the point of inevitable failure. This will destroy your motivation. Be realistic and break tasks into manageable chunks. Don't set out to learn Alan Dawson's *Rudimental Ritual* in a day. Aim to learn the first four bars to the highest standard you can. Then the next day learn the next four bars. Each little success will spur you on, increasing the chance of your reaching the ultimate goal of playing the whole piece.

R—Relevant

I have certainly sat at the kit in the past to learn a set for a gig the next day, only to succumb to the desire to learn a tricky but totally unrelated foot ostinato. Two hours later, I suddenly realize I still don't know the set for the impending gig and my practice session is over! So keep focused on the relevant tasks that you need to achieve.

T—Time-based

An open-ended goal will often get overtaken by other flights of fancy or pressing issues. When setting a goal, set a clear deadline, even if one doesn't really exist. Let's go back to the *Rudimental Ritual*. Instead of deciding to learn the rudimental ritual at some point in time, pick a realistic time limit—for example four weeks—and then just go for it. This will keep you motivated and focused. It also allows you to plan how many sessions you will have in four weeks and what your mini-goals should be for each individual session.

8. Take breaks.

This may seem counterintuitive to some. After all, we are trying to achieve more, so taking time away from that task must surely slow us down. But the truth is that regular short breaks allow us to maintain a high level of concentration and focus on the task at hand. Breaks might include getting a drink, physical stretching, or just walking away from the drums for a minute. After this minute or two, you will return to the drums with renewed vigor. If on the other hand you slavishly sit at the kit for hours on end, not only might you suffer the physical ailments of an aching back or sore arms, but your mental capacity will diminish accordingly. The more time spent playing without a break, the lesser your overall productivity. What will suffer? Your timing, your focus on the material that you are practicing, your ability to remember parts, and even the speed at which you learn them.

SECRET 2: PRACTICE DIARY

Following in the footsteps of Secret 1, a practice diary is an effective tool to help you reach your goals, stay motivated, and track your success. We are often forced to keep logs in the course of our music education, but then we don't bother to keep this practice up into adulthood. You should.

Simple entries after every practice session might include:

1. medium-term goals,
2. short-term goals,
3. lesson diary,
4. practice review,
5. issues to address,
6. performance feedback,
7. exercise/rudiment of the week,
8. practice methods,
9. notes, and
10. practice schedule.

A log or diary makes it very easy to set goals, review progress, stick to the plan, and address any issues that arise. You could also set yourself sight-reading tasks or tasks off the beaten path that force you to approach things differently and help stimulate new ideas.

SECRET 3: RECORD YOURSELF

Drummers should frequently record themselves so they can learn from what they hear and see.

When booked for a session, drummers will turn up, play, and, best of all, get to hear the results at the end. It is at this point where you might cringe upon hearing your rushed drum fill, excessive ghost notes on the snare (which had seemed brilliant at the time), or lack of musicality. This could be costly at an expensive studio with a client who won't book you again. Don't wait until then to hear recordings of yourself playing.

You might also find yourself playing differently during these recording situations because of the pressure you're likely to place on yourself while these notes are being committed to some sort of permanent (and distributed) record.

A cheap and simple way to avoid this is to record yourself during practice sessions. Increasing numbers of drummers own home recording facilities as technology improves and prices become more affordable. The rise in home electronic drum kits has also made MIDI recording incredibly easy via DAWs (digital audio workstations) like Cubase, Logic Pro, and others.

But even if you can't afford the equipment for high-quality recordings, a simple microphone recorder or even a mobile phone recorder will still allow you to capture the sound and review it. Here you can actually hear what you play, how well your limbs lock together, whether you rush fills or slow down after a fill, and all the other common mistakes that drummers commit without realizing it.

Once you have identified these weaknesses, you can correct them, and next time you are in a professional recording facility your performance will improve because of it. The cumulative effect will also be present in your playing through your greater confidence in your own ability.

To take this a step further, you might consider adding a visual element. By videoing yourself playing or just practicing in front of a mirror, you will more easily identify physical aspects that might hinder your performance or even cause injury.

Seeing your posture lets you identify perhaps the fact that you lean to one side (which can lead to spine discomfort). You might note that your arm movements are unnatural or you seem stiff, that you are wasting effort in moving around the kit. It might also help you optimize your kit setup by identifying problems in your equipment, problems that slow you down as you move across the drums.

This simple secret allows you to greatly improve your performances and ensure a professional job when that expensive studio clock is ticking.

SECRET 4: RHYTHM THEN ORCHESTRATION

Secrets 4 through 6 all focus on breaking down difficult passages and perfecting them at each stage before moving on. Taking the time through these sequences will not only enable you to reach the goal of playing the whole passage in less time, it will also ensure that you are executing the phrases with complete accuracy and natural feel.

Let's start with the figure below. We can see that the fill is fairly complex, both in the rhythm of the phrases as well as the orchestration around the drum kit.

I have seen too many drummers frantically attempt the entire passage at lightning speeds because they know how exciting it can sound. More often than not, however, the passage collapses in a mess of unwieldy notes. The drummers then attempt the exact same passage, again and again and again. Frustration grows, and the drummers feel dejected enough to abandon the passage altogether, returning to the safe ground of playing something they already know. Not only have they not achieved what they sought to learn; they have also built up an idea in their heads that they are just not good enough to play this passage of music.

But the truth is that they are more than capable. They simply took the wrong approach. Of course the first thing they should have done was to slow the whole passage down until it was manageable. But even then there are tips to take this to the next stage.

Figure 1.1.

If this entire passage seems daunting at first, a simple first step is to remove the orchestration around the kit and treat it purely from a rhythm perspective. Approach the phrase as if it were played entirely on a snare drum or practice pad. This allows you to focus on just the rhythm.

It is also a good idea at this point to work out how you'll count the rhythm. In most cases, if you can say it, you can play it. So sing the rhythm with counting before even trying it with sticks.

Once you've worked through this, pick the sticks up and count the rhythm while also playing it. You should find that your hands will naturally follow the counted rhythm. Repeat this exercise until it becomes almost subconscious.

When you have reached this stage it is time to work out the orchestration. But now you can fully focus on which drums to play the rhythm on, as you'll have already learned the rhythm itself. You may also want to consider the most sensible sticking pattern, but we'll discuss that in a later chapter.

Finally you can bring in the required dynamics.

SECRET 5: ADD A NOTE

Another approach is to break the passage down into single notes. Rather than looking at the passage as one large scary fill, treat it as lots of single notes.

The idea here is to treat this phrase at a very slow speed, one note at a time, in order to learn the mechanics and techniques needed to achieve that speed. The drum kit offers us the challenge of coordinating all four limbs, a challenge not generally faced by performers using other instruments. Therefore we must work on both the independence and coordination of the limbs at a very slow tempo until they lock together and the notes are evenly spaced.

We will use the same example as in Secret 4.

1. Set the metronome at the required speed and play the first note. If you are right-handed, then this will most likely be a right-hand note. Focus on the tone being played in the center of the snare drum with a clean rebound. Also consider if the note should bounce high in readiness of the next right-handed note or if it should stay low for a ghost note.
2. Repeat the first note until the movement and tone are perfect and the right hand is in position for its next note.
3. Once note one is perfect, add note two. Make sure the timing between the two notes is perfect and it flows naturally.
4. Add the third note, which is a new drum and a new limb.
5. Repeat the three notes until perfect in timing, feel, and dynamics.
6. Continue until the whole phrase is learned with perfect execution.

The first note is very simple here, but it is important not to buzz and to finish the stroke in the correct position, which is actually high up, making it a full stroke, to be ready for the first note of beat two. The second note would then be a left hand, which should also end high, ready for the second note of beat two on the high tom. Move it across there as soon as the snare has been played.

The next two notes are right foot bass drums. As you add these one at a time you will need to consider the suitable foot technique to allow flawless timing and consistency of power. Really take the time to make sure the timing is perfect between the three limbs before moving on.

As you move through the passage, you have the challenging movement of the sextuplet. Again, focus on timing, technique, and sticking in order to move around the kit in the most effective way. Are you holding tension in your grip? Is the transition between note values absolutely perfect? Are the dynamics accentuated enough? Are you finishing each note and naturally moving into position for the next note? Which hand should lead the flam? Are you moving from the double strokes in bar two into the double-handed triplet smoothly?

Consider each stage and only when you are satisfied that it sounds perfect should you continue to add a note.

The crucial thing here is to make sure that each stage is possible with total ease. If you are tense or straining with the last added note, then stay at that stage until you are relaxed enough to move on. This will ensure a perfect execution at the end. If the entire exercise is too challenging in one go, then separate it into smaller, more manageable chunks.

Hand and Foot Separation

Of course the drum kit is an instrument that requires mastery of all four limbs, so here is another example that creates some more challenges.

Figure 1.2.

I will often approach such a passage from multiple angles. The add-a-note approach will certainly be beneficial here, but I might first take the time to work out each limb, or at least sets of limbs, first.

The most obvious breakdown here is to split the hands and feet. It pays dividends later if you first work out the two patterns individually before embarking on an add-a-note approach or even trying the entire passage in one go.

First I would look at the hand pattern and the awkward three-note movement between the drums until the final four-note snare drum phrase. Again, consider the most appropriate sticking pattern and play it until you barely have to think about it. Now it's time to tackle the feet. You might notice that the hi-hat pedal is playing quarter notes while the bass drum starts halfway though beat one with a dotted eighth note feel. Play these individual elements until they feel comfortable and you are prepared enough to move on to the next approach and learn the entire passage by adding one note at a time. This dual approach will ultimately help achieve the end goal quicker.

SECRET 6: LOOPING

Having learned a difficult passage through the processes outlined in Secrets 4 and 5, and any other approaches that a drummer finds helpful, many drummers sit back satisfied that they have mastered the pattern.

Unfortunately this is not the case. To have mastered it, you must be able to play it with total ease at a range of tempos to a standard satisfactory to be heard on a professional stage. You will be able to transition from the pattern into another pattern and back again. You will be able to adapt the pattern, embellish it, take parts away, and anything else that might occur in a creative situation. This then gives you the total control and flexibility required to use this phrase in a musical context. Until you reach that level, you are still in the learning stages.

There is a process to go through to reach this stage that cannot be rushed. Different phrases and patterns will reach this stage quicker than others. What we are really trying to achieve here is to be "in the groove." Although difficult to define, most drummers will understand this phrase, just as an athlete strives to become "in the zone." It is a higher level of consciousness that is the product of a cyclic rhythm, whose components and nuances come together in such an emotive way that performers can lose themselves in the music that they are creating.

When you first grasp a rhythm and begin to play it as a loop, it will most likely not groove. The notes will be in the right order and technically it will be correct, but it will lack something. It might sound stiff or forced; your mind will be concentrating on which limb follows which and trying to consciously perform the dynamics appropriately.

If you think you are playing it correctly, it often helps to record yourself as mentioned in Secret 3. Now listen back and use a completely objective ear to determine if the quality of the drumming is good enough to be on a professional recording. If it's not, then you are not ready yet.

If you continue to play the pattern for long enough, and accurately enough, it will eventually drift into your subconscious and the rhythm will feel perfect.

Let's look at this rhythm example.

Figure 1.3.

It is not overly difficult, but difficult enough to have to think about the limbs and when they should play.

When learning this pattern, you might want to get used to the hi-hats on their own first, making sure the fourth sixteenth note open hi-hat of each beat is comfortable. I might even be inclined to learn them as straight sixteenth notes initially. You may wish to learn each bar individually and then bring them together later. We could then add the snares to this quite easily. The bass drums are the final element and these will cause the most difficulty. The syncopation and mechanics of lifting and dropping the feet will take a little work for most people. Think about each bass drum and where it falls in relation to an open hi-hat.

Now you have the complete pattern, you will need to play it slowly. Don't rush through this stage in an effort to reach the required tempo. We should instead focus on getting this to groove. It is here that I would start to bring in the swung sixteenth element, if it is not already present. Keeping it very slow, really focus on the hi-hats swinging. As you play the pattern, focus on the bass drums and hi-hats really locking together perfectly. Are any of them flamming? Could they be more accurate? If so, fix it now and continue to loop.

Even though we are at a slow tempo, I like to lose myself in the rhythm here. Rather than thinking of this as an annoying temporary speed that is part of a process to get somewhere better, really enjoy the rhythm that you are creating. Try to really feel this powerful, slow, swinging beat. Maybe you could sing a bass line or melody in your head as accompaniment. Try to make this pattern as musical as can be and just let it simmer for a while.

After some time, you might become aware that it is totally grooving; great. If you want to, keep playing and enjoying it. But if you wish to step it up, you are also ready. Don't suddenly jump up to full tempo. Take the metronome up five or ten bpm, and repeat the pattern until it is totally in the groove again. Make sure the limbs are locked together, the open hi-hats are clean, the dynamics are consistent. This pattern doesn't include any real variation in dynamics, but a pattern with ghost notes and accents will also need extra attention to make sure this aspect is optimized.

Repeat this process until full speed is attained. The key is making sure each stage is accurate and has that natural, flowing groove. Enjoy each process and be as musical as possible with it. By the time you reach the end goal, your groove will be totally embedded in you and this will shine through to the listeners when you perform it.

SECRET 7: DON'T FORGET TO BREATHE

Surely this is not a secret; we must all breathe instinctively or we wouldn't be alive to read this book. But it's surprising how many people stop breathing when they approach a difficult phrase on the drum kit.

Throughout our development we strive to play without tension, in a totally relaxed and natural state. And yet when we approach that tricky drum fill at a gig, that we only execute perfectly 50 percent of the time in practice, we hold our breath, tense up, and try to force the fill from our stiff, deprived muscles. This is denying our body of the thing it needs most: oxygen. Without it, our muscles are robbed of their fuel and the heart works faster. If you allow your lungs to completely empty, an accumulation of toxins will occur in your bloodstream so you will feel short of breath even when you breathe again. The same result will occur if you take an intake of breath when there is still air in your lungs as the new oxygen will sit upon the carbon dioxide beneath it.

This will affect your mental concentration as well as physical capability. Try holding your breath while playing some frantic drum fills. You might find that your notes are stiff or you are rushing to get to the end, and your mind will definitely be distracted so you won't be lost in the moment.

Now fill your lungs with a deep breath; allow yourself to get in a cycle of deep, slow intakes of breath and then exhalations. Now try playing again and you should feel much more relaxed and capable.

As drummers we don't need our mouths to play, unless we are someone like Phil Collins who sings and drums. But generally we are free to breathe at a steady rate while simultaneously drumming. We should not breathe in bursts between difficult phrases. We should instead keep a constant cycle going, just as we might when exercising; drumming is physical after all.

This can be solved with conscious thought. If I ever catch myself not breathing, I consciously take deep, slow breaths of air. I instantly feel my whole body relax and drumming becomes easier. This can become part of your practice routine, by playing various drum patterns while simultaneously focusing on deep, slow breaths. You may find this quite meditative, which will keep you calm if you transfer it to gig scenarios.

To aid this further, you might want to examine whether you could develop better technique, set your kit up more ergonomically, or play with less tension, as discussed in Secret 33.

SECRET 8: BEST STICKING

To return to the scenario in Secret 4, we drummers often rush into learning a new drum pattern head on. My advice thus far has centered on breaking down the parts and slowing down the speed to achieve the end result more quickly and less stressfully.

Another consideration when facing a new pattern should be the most appropriate sticking pattern to take you around the drums as required.

Sometimes this is instantly clear. If we were playing four sixteenth notes on the snare, high tom, mid tom, and floor tom, we would glide around effortlessly with a single stroke roll. But often the easiest way to move around the kit is not so obvious.

Discovering the best sticking pattern could make the difference between a jittery, uneven fill and a perfectly even, flawless one. And the quicker we discover this sticking pattern, the sooner we can enjoy that perfect execution and stop getting frustrated.

In many cases there is no single best sticking pattern, and we may find several options that do the same job. It may then be a question of which option comes most naturally for you. But as an exercise you may also want to try the other available options until they are just as good, purely for self-improvement.

Let's take the example below.

Figure 1.4.

The starting point for most drummers will be the single stroke roll. Although this would work at slow speeds, if we were to take this to high speeds, we would find certain areas difficult.

The snare at the start of beat two would involve crossing the right hand back over our left hand as it finishes the floor tom at the end of beat one. We would then have to bring the left back to the snare underneath the right as it plays that note. The final two notes would also be a challenge as the right hand plays the snare on the penultimate note and the left would then awkwardly cross over to the floor tom, meaning our right hand is trapped and unable to move toward a crash cymbal ready to return to our drum groove.

As mentioned, this would seriously inhibit a fast, smooth execution and so we may want to look at alternatives. And it is here that you will be glad of all those hours spent practicing rudiments throughout your drumming life!

You can see below that I have taken the same fill but split it into four phrases. This is just a suggested sticking, and you may find better patterns that suit you.

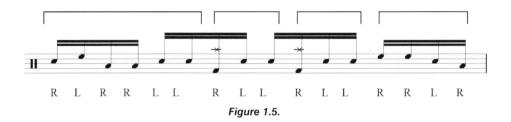

R   L   R   R   L   L   R   L   L   R   L   L   R   R   L   R

Figure 1.5.

The first six-note phrase is a paradiddle-diddle. This makes it very easy to move the doubles between the floor tom and snare drum.

The second and third phrase are right, left, left, with the right hand staying up on the crash while the left easily copes with two doubles on the snare.

The final phrase is an inverted paradiddle, simply to bring us out of the previous phrase and allow the move from high tom to snare to floor tom without crossing hands.

Try this sticking pattern slowly, as it will take some thought at first. But as you repeat it and get used to it, you will find that you are able to move through this fill with total ease.

Get in the habit of considering this aspect with every fill and beat that isn't instantly easy to play. Before long you will start to recognize patterns more quickly within the larger phrases and your hands will begin to find their way with less conscious thought. Ultimately you will save yourself a great deal of time and effort.

SECRET 9: AVOID THE RUT—HOW TO FIND INSPIRATION

Hearing drummers tell me that they have nothing to practice is one of the poorest excuses I can imagine and frankly one that astounds me as it shows a total lack of imagination. There is rhythm all around us if we are tuned in to it. The sound of the washing machine spinning around creates a cyclic rhythm, the indicator in my car gives me a metronome that gets me tapping (watch the road though!), and there is music being played all around us in shops, cafes, and vehicles.

But when we sit at the kit, many of us have found ourselves in a rut—unable to find any inspiration and simply going through the motions of playing the same old beats and fills that we know inside out.

The first thing I would suggest is reading Secret 1 and having a planned practice session in advance so you know which practice goals you need to achieve each week.

But beyond that, you should find your mind flooded with ideas if you follow these steps:

1. Force yourself to do something different.

Maybe you're a rock drummer. You love sticking on a Led Zeppelin CD and jamming along with Bonham. So why not stick on a Miles Davis CD today and play along with Tony Williams? Playing new styles out of your comfort zone will take you in new directions, give you new insight, and force you into different techniques and approaches, which can only aid your improvement as a drummer and help to give fresh inspiration.

2. Twist an old exercise.

Steve Gadd is a great example of a drummer who takes well-worn ideas and gives them a twist that breathes freshness and life into them, while creating exciting and mysterious-sounding ideas. One such example is the use of double strokes inverted and separated with bass drums in such tracks as "Chuck E's in Love" by Rickie Lee Jones and "Oh, Marion" by Paul Simon.

In figure 1.6 we can see the humble double stroke roll with the right hand on the hi-hat and the left hand on the snare. If we then displace that by one sixteenth note in the second line, we find that the doubles are still there but they are inverted so that we start with one right hand and then continue with two on each hand, with each hand change occurring on the second and fourth sixteenth note of each beat.

By line three we have then removed that single right hand at the beginning, as well as on the eighth note (the "a" of beat two). We have replaced these notes with bass drums. The second half of the bar is the same except for the first note of beat three being played on the snare with an accented right hand. We have also added a softer dynamic to the other snare drums.

Figure 1.6.

It's only a slight change from the starting point of a double stroke roll, but the resulting sound is unrecognizable as the initial rudiment. Try this pattern and hopefully you can apply a similar approach to many old rudiments, beats, and fills to recycle them and end up with something new and interesting.

3. Play open handed.

Another way to turn things on their heads is to swap your leading hand. If you are a right-handed drummer that normally plays with cross hands, try opening them up so the left hand plays the hi-hat and the right hand plays the snare. This approach can be seen in many great drummers, such as Carter Beauford, and allows them great freedom of movement around the kit. This is not just a silly way to fill practice time. This can help develop your ambidexterity and help you discover new groove and fill ideas as you find yourself moving differently on the kit.

4. Break rhythms into less obvious phrases.

Bill Bruford promotes this approach to create quirky rhythms within quite standard time signatures. Let's take a twelve/eight rhythm. We will naturally phrase this in two groups of six. Those six-note groups will then be divided into two groups of three with the bass drum on the first note and the snare drum on the fourth note. But how many other ways can we divide twelve? We could have a phrase of five and a phrase of seven. Or maybe a four, five, and three phrase. See figure 1.7 to get an idea of this. Once you have developed these phrases, think about how you could orchestrate them around the kit. Why not look at other common rhythm types and try to phrase them differently?

Figure 1.7.

We spend much of our time forced to practice specific parts for a gig, rehearsal, audition, or exam; the opportunity to sit at the kit and just play becomes very precious. Embrace that opportunity and use it to discover something new.

SECRET 10: PLAY MORE WITH LESS

As young drummers, most of us look at the monstrous drum kits of Nicko Mc-Brain, Joey Jordison, Terry Bozzio, and Thomas Lang with burning envy. We then set about trying to build the size of our kit with anything that makes a sound, regardless of sound quality or any practical implications.

This lets us explore our imagination and is great fun (until we have to start moving it for gigs), but it can also inhibit our musicality, expression, and imagination as we develop as drummers.

A drummer who has seven toms will often feel inspired, and maybe even obligated in order to justify these toms, to play long rolls around those drums from top to bottom. The subdivisions might not change very often and the patterns become recognizable rather quickly. All this equipment means that this drummer doesn't feel the need to be creative by stretching his ideas because he has so many loud, different-sounding things to hit all around him.

So as an exercise strip your kit back to a classic jazz style four piece: bass, snare, one rack tom, and one floor tom. Of the cymbals, keep only hi-hat and ride, and maybe one crash if you really want to.

If you are used to a larger kit, you will instantly feel exposed and vulnerable. Good. This exercise is designed to squeeze out your musical ideas and maximize your creativity. The drum kit is one of the most expressive instruments in the world. Take the hi-hat: how many different dynamics and timbres can you achieve from this alone? Play it on the edge, halfway in, at the center. Use the tip of your stick; now use the shoulder. Close the hi-hat tight, open it to the full, and everything in between. How many sounds does your snare drum offer? Strike it in the middle, at the edge. Play cross stick; play a rim shot. Push your hand into the skin while hitting it with a stick to bend the pitch. Play it very soft; play it very loud. Play a buzz roll. It is so expressive. Go around each part of the kit and take the time to explore its potential. Think hard about how you can play it, how you can modify its sound, and what you can get out of it.

Now that you have explored the possibilities of each sound source, let's put this into practice. Let's now create a drum solo. Read Secret 50 for some thematic and melodic ideas if you need inspiration.

Let's begin by creating a drum solo that lasts for one minute and consists only of snare drum. Use every sound and dynamic that you discovered when exploring this drum. Squeeze out as much as you can in terms of expression and musicality. Bring the drum to life and create excitement with it. It might have quite a military feel, like a marching drummer. Explore the masters of that style of drumming to see how they use stick clicks, rims, and snares to create interest.

Next repeat this exercise with just the hi-hat. Study players like Buddy Rich to see how great a hi-hat solo can be. Listen to how expressive this voice is. Repeat for each part of the drum kit.

Now create a drum solo and make it the most musical, interesting, and inspired piece of music that you have ever created. Don't think of the drum kit as a loud, crashing, Neanderthal tool, but as a musical instrument that can convey emotion. You might surprise yourself. You may also find it impossible to go back to your elongated, thoughtless tom rolls!

If you repeat this kind of exercise, you will definitely grow as a drummer and build confidence in your ability to express something on the drum kit. And if you adopt this setup for live work instead of your fifteen-piece kit of the past, you will also save yourself a great deal of money on chiropractor fees as a bonus.

CHAPTER 2

Technique Strategies

SECRET 11: PLAY WITHOUT TENSION

I see many drummers with great musicality and ability holding themselves back by ignoring their technique. They are inhibiting their potential and making things harder than they need to be by failing to harness the energy of the drumstick. As well as a detriment to your playing, poor technique can cause physical injury that could force you to stop drumming. (These risks of physical injury are discussed in Secret 34.)

One of the most serious problems I see in students is the tension they hold onto while playing. That is very easily retained and often without your realizing it. Once you learn how to remove this tension, you can play not only at a higher level but with less effort.

Here are some areas to focus on, as well as exercises to help free you of tension.

Breathing

As discussed in Secret 7, many drummers forget to breathe when they concentrate too hard or find themselves playing difficult parts.

Conscious attention to the matter can solve this problem. Whenever I catch myself not breathing, I consciously take deep, slow breaths of air. I instantly feel my whole body relax and my drumming become easier. This should become part of your practice routine. When you play various drum patterns, focus simultaneously on taking deep, slow breaths.

Tension

We must assess whether there is tension in our body when we play. If you sit at the kit with sticks in position ready to play, you might well find that, upon considering it, you feel tense. That tension might be in your wrist, your forearm, your shoulders, your neck, or even your lower back. Try to relax the part of your body that is tense. Breathe deep and slow. Notice the tension pour out of you, but make sure you maintain good posture and don't allow a spine slump to occur.

Exercise 1

Once you sense that you are tension-free, try playing a slow single stroke roll on the snare drum. As you play the notes, maintain the regular breathing and relaxed muscles. Play as smoothly as you can. Listen carefully to the notes to make sure they are even. It might help if you close your eyes to remove distractions, increase awareness, and help focus the mind.

Once you get a feel for this relaxed playing, you might find that as you increase speed and volume, the tension returns. It is important that you consciously introduce this approach to all tempos and dynamics. Try to simply play notes from a greater distance to achieve a louder dynamic instead of tensing your wrist and crashing down with more force onto the drum. When playing fast, tension will inhibit you, so it is even more important to stay loose and relaxed.

Bearing the previous paragraph in mind, try playing very fast single stroke rolls while focusing on being as loose as possible. Keep breathing slowly, close your eyes, and consciously relax your arms, shoulders, and wrists. You will also need to consider different grips here, which is discussed later in this section. Once you find the point where tension creeps in, drop the tempo slightly until you are relaxed again. Check the bpm and aim to push the relaxed rolls up a few bpms each week.

Movement Pattern

The final thing to assess is the actual movement pattern that you make when playing a note. Play a single stroke on the snare drum with the right hand. Assess the movement of the arm and wrist. Is it in a straight rigid line from elbow to tip of stick? Repeat with the left hand.

This rigid, straight-line playing makes extremely hard work of drumming and also means that most of the shock when the stick hits the head is being absorbed by the arm. This can cause injury, so we need to use that energy to play the next note rather than absorbing it and then having to find more of our own energy to play the next note.

Exercise 2

As the arm rises for the back lift, the wrist should go limp, allowing it to hang down (figure 2.1). As the arm reaches the apex of its movement, the wrist then straightens out, allowing the stick to flick back slightly beyond the straight-line position (figure 2.2), ready to whip down and play the note.

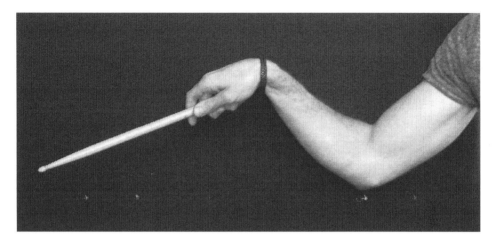

Figure 2.1.

Figure 2.2.

This allows a much more natural and relaxed movement for the body and also enables us to produce greater speed and power from our movement. To achieve this movement, there can be no tension at all in that limb.

Evaluate each of the above aspects to help you remove all tension when playing and pursue your optimum level.

Of course, to keep your body relaxed, the position of the drums and cymbals is very important. This is discussed in Secret 33.

SECRET 12: THE BOUNCE

Now that you are free of tension, we must look more deeply into getting the most from the energy of the stick to create multiple notes with each downstroke. If we physically had to play every note by lifting our arm up and bringing it back down, we would struggle to play with much speed at all. This motion requires a great deal of energy and time.

So instead we rely greatly on our fast, small finger muscles, as well as the natural bounce of the drumstick, which occurs every time it hits a solid object, such as a drumhead.

Many beginning drummers prevent this natural bounce from occurring through a stiff grip and lack of technique. They then have to start from scratch to generate the power for the next note: a great waste of time and effort.

This secret looks at harnessing the bounce of the stick and using the fingers to control the subsequent notes.

We will focus on two key aspects here: using the fingers and wrists and allowing the bounce to occur.

Allowing the Bounce to Occur

The number one, most important thing here is to allow the stick to bounce up after you've struck the drum. You should absolutely not pull the stick up at all; it should rise to its starting position by its own steam.

Exercise 1

Imagine a basketball player bouncing a ball. He pushes the ball down toward the floor, and it bounces back into his hand. In no way does he lift the ball back up to his hand; he simply allows it to naturally bounce back and then rises with the ball as he reconnects with it, rather than allowing it to smack into a solid hand. He moves with the ball and uses its energy.

In this exercise we need to focus on this same bounce. Starting with your stick raised toward the ceiling (figure 2.3), throw it down toward your practice pad to play a note. Keeping your hand around the stick, allow it to bounce back to the start position (figure 2.4). Do not help it bounce back; simply move your hand with it until it is pointing toward the ceiling.

It can take some getting used to the fine balance of allowing the stick to bounce while keeping control and guiding it so it doesn't fly off and end up in somebody's eye.

Figure 2.3.

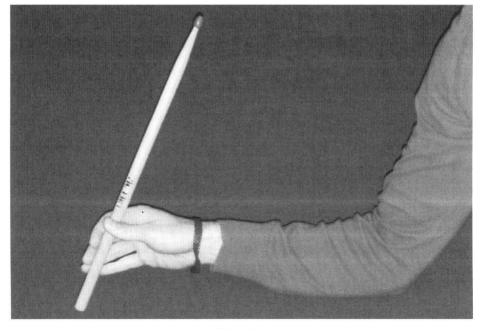

Figure 2.4.

But once mastered, you are now ready for the next note and don't need an up-stroke to get there; you are already there!

Once you get a feel for this, you can play continuous notes. Make sure you work on both hands individually at first.

Exercise 2

The action for these notes is almost entirely wrist and fingers. This exercise aims to help focus on the correct motions by eliminating all arm movement above the wrist. Although not a natural way to play, as an exercise it helps us get a feel for the correct movements and forces us to use the bounce rather than lifting the arm.

Here we are going to play a continuous single stroke roll on the practice pad. There should be no arm movement whatsoever.

To ensure this, lay a piece of wood across the top of your wrists (such as two drumsticks taped together) in order to isolate the wrist movement. If you were to move an arm, the taped stick would fall off its perch.

Once you get a feel for this, try playing other groupings and stickings. Try with each hand double strokes, paradiddles, or groups of three, the first being an accent followed by two bounces. Maybe increase these groups to four, and then five, and so on, to see how far you can get. If you repeat this regularly, you will find that you can complete these notes with great ease and control.

Using the Fingers to Control the Bounce

Exercise 3

This exercise is designed to increase awareness of the fingers and to develop their involvement. You might wish to adopt something close to the French grip for this (see Secret 13).

Here we will play continuous notes just using one finger at a time. This helps build awareness of each finger's role.

Hold the stick in the right-hand fulcrum as usual and play continuous notes using only the little finger to play each note. All the other fingers should not be involved.

Now repeat the exercise using only the ring finger, then only the middle finger, and finally the index finger. Now complete the same warm-up with the left hand.

Once you get a feel for this, try different groups to develop the control even further. First play four sixteenth notes with each finger on the right hand, moving up through them as we did before. Aim for the transition between each finger to be seamless. Always repeat on the left hand. Now try groups of triplets with each finger. Then try doubles, and finally move through singles.

The final stage is to try interleaving both hands to create a single stroke roll. Working through the single hand exercises that we just discussed, try four sixteenth notes with your little finger alternating between right and left; so right little finger (RLF), left little finger (LLF), RLF, LLF, RLF, LLF, RLF, LLF. Then repeat this alternating roll with the ring finger, middle finger, and index finger.

Then try the same sequence playing triplets, doubles, and finally singles.

SECRET 13: WHICH GRIP?

Many drummers consider themselves to be a single-grip player: traditional or matched. While this might tell part of the story, I believe that by really developing and considering the different gripping options, we can find easier ways to perform each pattern and do so for an entire, gruelling performance.

Both matched and traditional grips are very old as seen on European drums such as the nakers, which were often used with matched grip in the 13th century. When the pipe and tabor, and nakers, gave way to the larger, heavier field drum by the late 15th century, a new grip was needed to allow the left hand to play over the elevated rim of the drum. The left hand therefore adopted an almost backward grip that we now call traditional grip. Once we hit the 1960s, drummers were competing with loud guitar amps and the emergence of rock music, so they adopted the matched grip to enable more power on the snare drum.

Since then, a broad generalization might be that lighter players, such as those who play jazz, use traditional grip. Heavier players use the matched grip. It might be suggested that traditional grip might not be as good for our technique, posture, and likelihood of injury, but conversely many of the greatest drummers of all time play traditional grip: Buddy Rich, Dave Weckl, Vinnie Colaiuta, and Steve Gadd, to name just four.

Your grip preference will most likely have been dictated by several factors such as guidance from your tutors, favored performance genre, and personal preference in what feels comfortable.

But the purpose of this chapter is to discuss multigrip playing. I personally find that sometimes if I play jazz, I naturally adopt a traditional grip as it helps me play at a lower dynamic when comping, and also possibly because it subconsciously gets me in the right frame of mind.

So we may find that grip decisions are made depending on the situation, playing style, and required dynamic level.

But even if choosing one grip, we can vary how we use that grip. Let's take matched grip for example. I use this for a majority of my playing. But within that umbrella classification, I will adopt German, French, and American grips to aid various applications.

French grip (figure 2.7) sees the thumb on top of the stick and great use of the fingers to play a note. This allows a lighter tone, lower dynamic control, and greater dexterity, so faster phrases might be best suited to this grip. German grip (figure 2.8) uses the palms facing down and a wrist action that allows more power and a darker tone, but sometimes at the expense of dexterity. This then might be used for heavy backbeats. American grip (figure 2.9) is very popular with drum kit players, as it is very similar to German but sees the elbows come in a little, so it's more relaxed, and subsequently the wrist turns so that the hand position is somewhere between French and German.

As well as our grip being determined by the style, each hand may alter individually depending what and where on the kit we are playing. I also find that I might vary my grips throughout a performance to help avoid fatigue. If my hand becomes tired, I will turn the wrist slightly to use the muscles differently and give myself some relief.

Exercise 1

Here we are playing a heavy rock beat as far as the bass drum and snare drum are concerned, but more of a samba style right-hand pattern on the ride cymbal. To obtain that accented snare drum, the left hand might adopt the German grip here. But for the lighter and more intricate cymbal pattern, you might choose a French grip for the left hand. Try this pattern using the suggested grips.

Figure 2.5.

Exercise 2

Here we are using the same pattern as in Exercise 1 with the addition of a bell accent on the eighth note ride cymbals, creating a "ding-tata ding-tata" type sound. Here you might adopt a right-hand technique that allows this change in dynamic as well as moving from the main body of the cymbal to the bell with minimal fuss.

This involves playing the accented ride bell with a German grip, and then turning your wrist to play the last two sixteenth notes of each beat with a French grip. This twisting allows movement on and off of the bell very easily, as well as giving the power for the accent.

Figure 2.6. French Grip

This technique is also very helpful for increasing speed for up-tempo jazz or samba patterns, which are essentially the same on the ride.

Figure 2.7. French Grip

Figure 2.8. German Grip

Figure 2.9. American Grip

SECRET 14: FUNDAMENTAL BASS TECHNIQUES

In Secret 13 we looked at different stick grips and how each one can benefit certain types of playing. This section examines some fundamental bass drum pedal techniques that are available to our feet. I believe that a good understanding of these main techniques is essential in order to play with maximum control and ease.

It is important to note that there is no wrong or right here and there is no "one size fits all" technique. This really is a case of each individual performer finding what works for him or her, but also being au fait with several techniques in order to employ the most suitable technique for each different exercise.

Before even looking at the feet, it is important to ensure a good seating position, as discussed in Secret 33.

Once you are positioned correctly, you have a few choices to make, such as which part of the pedal to use, whether to leave the beater buried in the drumhead or not, and whether the heel should be raised or not. Here we will discuss these options.

Heel Down

This technique sees us resting our entire foot on the pedal board, which allows the beater to rebound very naturally. Therefore this creates a more resonant tone that might suit an open-sounding bass drum, like that found in many jazz situations. It also enables great dynamic control at lower levels, so again is well suited to quieter styles such as jazz.

Here we are playing from the ankle so we sacrifice the power of the leg muscles, and therefore this style is often ignored where loud, punchy bass drums are needed

Figure 2.10.

such as rock, pop, and funk. Many drummers also struggle to play with any great speed using this technique, although players such as Colin Bailey demonstrate this to be highly possible, as seen in his DVDs and books.[1]

Heel Up

This technique is favored by many players in styles such as rock, pop, funk, metal, and anywhere else a loud, punchy bass drum sound is required. As the name suggests, the heel is raised off the pedal and the contact is made by the front part of the foot. This allows much more force to be applied to the pedal through the leg muscles bearing down on it.

The power comes from the thigh here, rather than the ankle as seen in the heel down technique. As well as this increased power, many drummers find this technique conducive to faster playing. By utilizing ankle and foot movements, multiple notes can be achieved with only a single whole leg movement.

Here the player will usually find part of the pedal that responds most efficiently to the force they apply on it. This is known as the sweet spot.

Because the leg weight comes down on the pedal, the beater is often left buried in the head after each note. This prevents optimum resonance but is often seen as inconsequential, as the playing styles often dictate that the bass drum is heavily muffled anyway. Some players like to rest the heel on the foot plate after each note to allow more resonance.

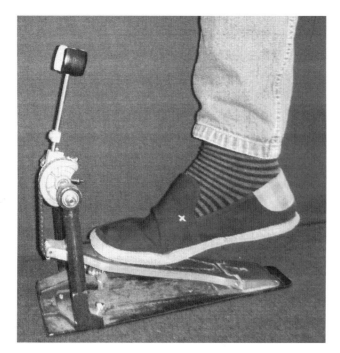

Figure 2.11.

Slide/Pivot

This technique is very popular for achieving great speed while maintaining power. Just as we have discussed the bounce of the stick to achieve more notes with less effort, this technique looks to create two notes from a single movement. When playing two consecutive notes at high speed, the act of lifting the thigh for each note takes time and energy.

The slide sees us playing a note with the foot further down the pedal. The note will be played with the very front of the foot (figure 2.12). After playing this note the foot should rise slightly, which allows the pedal to naturally begin bouncing back. The foot only lifts enough to allow this pedal movement to occur and does not rise completely off the pedal.

As this is taking place, the foot then slides slightly forward, connecting with the pedal across the ball of the foot, which causes a second note to be played (figure 2.14).

This allows us to play two notes while only lifting the leg once. The additional movement for note two is made from the ankle down, only involving a slight forward slide motion and angle change of the foot.

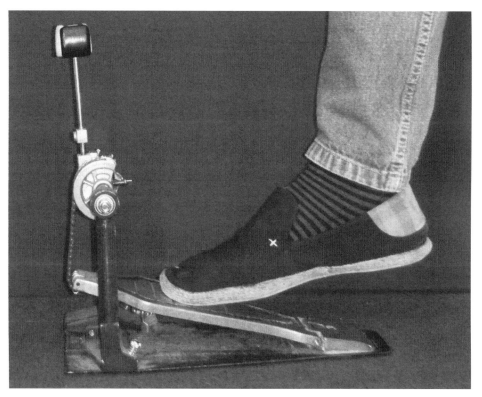

Figure 2.12.

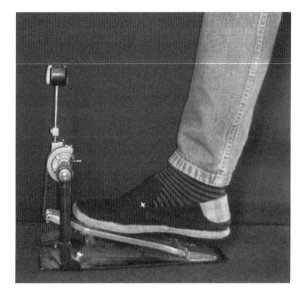

Figure 2.13.

Heel/Toe

This is an alternative to the slide/pivot technique. As mentioned, there's no single "best" technique; it's a case of finding your preference.

When playing two consecutive fast notes, you will play the first note much further toward the back of the foot plate. It is misleading to be called heel/toe as people often assume that the heel strikes the plate. This is not the case. The heel falls down on to the base of the foot plate, while the foot strikes the pedal about halfway down the foot board. The knee then immediately rises and the toes fall downward, using the ankle to control this, causing a second note to be played.

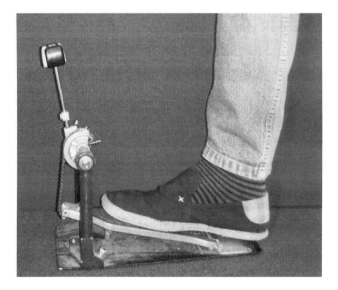

Figure 2.14.

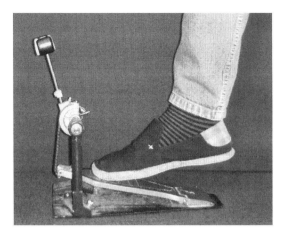

Figure 2.14a.

Flat Foot

This technique is regularly employed by fast double bass drum players, often found in the heavy metal genres. It utilizes the fast twitch muscles and very slight movements, with speed being the main objective.

The feet are positioned low down the footboard, which may seem counterintuitive as we are no longer on the sweet spot. The very front of the foot is the only part that makes contact with the lower part of the pedal, and the foot stays in this low position, parallel with the floor and therefore appearing flat (figure 2.15). The whole leg is used to play the notes but the movements are very slight. This vastly compromises power, although the problem is often solved with microphones and electronic triggers.

Figure 2.15.

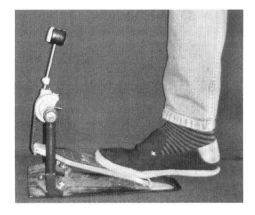

There are other techniques used on the bass drum, and many slight variations on the ones covered here, but a good understanding of these main techniques will enable you to shift between them to find the one most appropriate for each challenge you face.

SECRET 15: NATURE'S WAY

The forces of nature are all around us; whether it's the sea crashing against the shore or the wind hammering against the trees on a stormy day. The sheer power is impossible to ignore, and as drummers we are constantly working alongside or against these forces.

When we try to play faster notes, laws of physics dictate that there is a maximum speed at which we can play. We may find ways to push ourselves beyond our current threshold but ultimately, there is a maximum that we can achieve. When we try to create enough noise to be heard over the egotistical guitarist, who is pushing his amp to the limit, we also find a limit as to how hard we can actually hit the drum and how much sound it can produce.

And it is really these two aspects of speed and power that this secret is discussing. Many drummers are on a never-ending journey for more power and speed. Although this is something that is certainly more prevalent in younger, inexperienced drummers, older drummers may never lose sight of this goal in certain extreme genres. For many of us, as we gain more experience, we place more importance on choosing the right notes rather than playing lots of notes, just as we also look for greater quality of sound rather than just more sound.

As a result, many inexperienced musicians create a sound that is thin and lacking in power. The decision to add more notes in every beat and fill often takes away the sheer power that the track might have benefited from.

As drummers we must realize that our ability to create speed and power is finite, and in fact one restricts the other. It is inevitable that the faster the notes you play the more power you sacrifice. By playing fast rolls around the kit, you are unable to bring your stick back far enough to snap it down with a powerful accent to the same extent that you would if you played a single note.

So sometimes by playing less notes we can actually create a much bigger, weightier sound that will help the track sound much more effective and polished. It also allows your carefully chosen and well-tuned drums (see the "Equipment Strategies" chapter) to really sing and be heard.

One famous example of a fairly slow but very powerful drum groove is that by John Bonham on Led Zeppelin's "When the Levee Breaks." The space between notes allowed the huge reverb sound created by placing the drums at the bottom of a stairwell, which is an integral aspect of the track's sound and would have been impossible if Bonham was playing fast rolls throughout.

Also think about half-time grooves and how powerful they sound. Many heavy tracks feature a breakdown into a half-time section that sounds much bigger than the rest of the track. The extra space creates a more powerful sound.

Beating Nature

It is also worth noting at this stage that many drummers look for loopholes where speed versus power is concerned. One attempt to beat nature is through the use of triggers. Increasing numbers of drummers have adopted this technique, most predominantly in the heavy metal genres where so many fast notes are played.

The biggest use of triggers in this genre is on the bass drum. Due to the "boomy" nature of this big wooden cylinder, it can be difficult to achieve sufficient clarity when playing continuous fast notes, as exhibited by fast double bass drum metal playing. We also have the issue of loss of power, as discussed. Therefore triggers are attached to the drums that send a voltage signal through to a drum module that converts this signal into a note from a chosen drum sample, at a chosen volume.

Although the use of triggers does work in some situations, it is not a good choice for many styles, techniques, and settings. Therefore it is a useful exercise to develop your musicianship and drum composition skills so that you can create the perfect drum part every time.

Exercise 1

To experiment with this concept, try recording the drum part to a heavy song. Play as many notes in the fills as possible; play the grooves as frenetically and fast as possible. Now record again and play fewer notes but make them full and powerful. Think about the tones; consider slowing the groove down; play eighth note hi-hats instead of sixteenth notes; and so forth.

Now listen back to each recording and see which works the best. It might be the first, faster one, but often you will find that fewer, well-chosen notes will create the most pleasing result.

NOTE

1. Colin Bailey, *Bass Drum Technique*, DVD (2011); *Bass Drum Control* (Milwaukee, WI: Hal Leonard, July 1998); *Bass Drum Control Solos* (Milwaukee, WI: Hal Leonard, August 2002).

CHAPTER 3

Timing Strategies

SECRET 16: DEVELOPING YOUR INTERNAL METRONOME

To develop the necessary sense of timing that a professional drummer requires, you must develop your internal metronome. This helps a musician feel the space within the music, so that the notes he or she plays will be performed with confidence and precision.

A very effective exercise for developing this ability is to work on breaking down the empty space between notes so that you can count them internally. This helps divide a larger space in time into smaller units so that we don't get lost and panic when playing our next note.

Exercise 1

Set the metronome at a slow tempo. The slower tempos are much harder as the space between notes is larger. Begin at 50 bpm. These clicks will be treated as quarter notes (crotchets).

Using a single sound source such as a snare drum or practice pad, begin playing quarter notes, one for every metronome click. Depending on your experience and natural timing, this might be easy or seemingly impossible.

Now we will subdivide these quarter notes.

Circles of Time

The common method when playing these quarter notes is to move rapidly from the start position down toward the drumhead for impact before rebounding back to the start position equally rapidly in order to wait for the next note. These uneven, jerking movements can leave us lost in time, hurriedly stabbing at the drum and not feeling at ease with the metronome.

To help mark the space between the clicks, try moving your forearm, wrist, hand, and stick in a vertical circle, always maintaining an even speed that brings us comfortably round to the drum head for each impact with the click. It is crucial to move at a constant speed that brings the circle round exactly to meet the click. This constant motion enables us to feel that space much more naturally and therefore play the note much more accurately and confidently with each metronome click.

Exercise 2

Another exercise involves the drummer subdividing these quarter notes by counting smaller note values between them silently in his head. Continuing with the metronome at 50 bpm, count eighth notes (quavers) silently as 1 & 2 & 3 & 4 &. But play only the quarter notes (the numbers). This enables us to split the space between the quarter notes into two smaller units of time, which is then easier to feel. The next step involves dividing those quarter notes into sixteenth notes (semiquavers) by counting 1 e & a 2 e & a 3 e & a 4 e & a. We have now broken these units of time down even further to make the spaces more manageable.

Combine the counting with the circular motion, making sure to be at the top of the circle for the count of & on the eighth note, or at either side of the circle when playing sixteenth notes for the e and a count.

It is most beneficial to practice these techniques in a range of tempos from very slow to fast.

Exercise 3

Once you feel comfortable and in complete control with the previous exercises, you can progress by removing some of the metronome clicks.

Using a pre-recorded loop, or with the aid of a DAW through which you can loop a sample, set up a metronome to give quarter notes at 50 bpm for three beats with the fourth beat missing. Using the same methods as the previous exercises, play all four quarter notes.

With the last metronome click now missing, this larger gap leaves a two-beat gap between the third click on beat three and the next click on beat one of the next bar. This requires you to use your newly developed internal metronome to accurately and confidently hit beat four without the reassurance of the metronome to guide you. Only when the next beat is played on beat one of the next bar will you know if you are staying in time. When you have developed the internal metronome sufficiently from the previous exercise, you will execute that note perfectly.

Once this feels natural, set the metronome to play two quarter notes, leaving a three-beat gap in each bar. Then extend the gap to four beats. If you are able to stay consistently in time with only one click in each bar, then you have reached a very high level indeed.

Exercise 4

The next step to building your internal metronome is to use these techniques in a more musical context.

Move to the drum kit. Using the metronome loop with the missing beats, set it up with a two-bar loop. The first bar will be complete with four quarter note clicks. The second bar will have only three clicks with beat four missing.

See figure 3.1. For the first bar you will play a simple groove. For this exercise, I have used a standard rock beat. The second bar consists of the same groove for three beats with a space on beat four where the click is missing. Over this beat you must improvise a fill. This is an extension of the previous exercises as you will now have the whole drum kit at your disposal and the added uncertainty of improvising a fill.

Make sure you transition into and back out of the fill with perfect timing and no need for adjustment when you return to the groove.

Once this becomes comfortable, increase the gap in bar two to a two-beat gap (2), missing beats three and four. Then extend it to three beats (3) and finally the entire bar (4).

Figure 3.1.

When you have practiced each of these exercises sufficiently and sense that you are in complete control of your internal metronome, move on to Secret 17: Master of the Metronome.

SECRET 17: MASTER OF THE METRONOME

Building on Secret 16, you should now be reasonably confident about playing in time with a metronome at a range of tempos. You should also feel less a slave to the click and more in control of your own timing. This chapter helps take that feeling to the next stage so that you are the master of that metronome completely.

Exercise 1

First of all, let's see if you can play with total accuracy on the click. Set it for 50 bpm, so it is slow and challenging, and simply play a basic rock beat. If beats one and three consist of a hi-hat and bass and beats two and four a snare and hi-hat, then we are aiming for those kit voices to completely eliminate the metronome's click. If you play exactly at the same time, you will not hear the click. This might seem strange at first, but don't panic; the metronome hasn't broken. You are perfectly in time with it.

Although this now feels like we have mastered the click, if we look to more experienced musicians, we find that they have the freedom to move around that metronome at will in order to create different feels and moods within the music. They do not always sit directly on top of each click.

A laid-back track might involve a slightly behind-the-beat rhythm, whereas a fast, attacking track might see the drummer playing ahead of the beat.

Many of us have a natural feel that sees us subconsciously ahead, behind, or on top of the beat. But if we can learn to harness control of this timing, then we can create any feel at any given time. We might even change timing within the same song, spending a laid-back verse playing behind the beat, then transitioning into a frenzied chorus that requires us to play in front of the beat.

Below are some exercises to help develop this timing control.

Exercise 2

This will go against all your instincts now that you have developed such metronomic precision, but take the time with this exercise and it will make sense. With the click at a slow tempo again, play the same rock beat from Exercise 1. Allow your notes to fall slightly behind each click, so that they create what we call a flam between yourself and the click. Resist the temptation to land back on the click, but also keep the notes steady. The hi-hats should maintain perfectly even eighth notes, all equally behind the clicks. Repeat this pattern until it becomes comfortable. This might not happen in one practice session so be prepared to revisit this exercise numerous times.

Exercise 3

Now we repeat this exercise playing in front of the click. This time try to push slightly ahead so that flam is created again, but this time you play first so the click follows. Whether behind or ahead, try to see how far back, or in front, you can push that beat before you lose it. The aim is to hold it there consistently so your rhythm still sounds great to the listeners. They will be unaware of any metronome, but will subconsciously respond to the feel that you have created with respect to the other musicians.

Exercise 4

Now that you have mastered the feel of playing a basic drumbeat on, behind, and in front of the click, it is time to move away from that safety net. Now try to add fills, vary the drum pattern, introduce sixteenth beats, and so on. Get creative, just as you would at a live performance. Make sure you maintain the chosen feel at all times. Also experiment with switching between different feels, as mentioned earlier, so that you can vary the tension between sections of a song.

This will also help your timing in general so you should find it even easier now to play right on the click. Your sense of space in the music, and your effect on the feel, will increase drastically, enabling you to make smart musical choices for the feel of each song.

SECRET 18: FIND YOUR ACHILLES' HEEL

When developing timing, most drummers will find a weak spot in their armory: an Achilles' heel. Even when they are sounding very solid and professional, this one aspect might show them to be less competent than first thought.

It is crucial for us to identify this area (or areas) as early as possible in order to correct it. One of the easiest ways to do this, other than taking constructive criticism from fellow musicians as part of the learning curve, is to record yourself. This was discussed in Secret 3, and it is still the best way to evaluate your playing.

If you have access to any of the numerous DAW software packages available for home studios today, then you should have an even easier job. Here, rather than using just your ears, you can see a visual representation of what you play set against a grid on the screen. Now we can know exactly which notes were in time and which were out of time at a glance.

Timing errors in drummers are most prevalent during the transition into and out of fills. The steady, consistent groove will sit fine but once we dare to move away from the safety of that repetition, reposition our body, stretch our limbs, and try to move around the drum kit, the timing often collapses. This can happen to varying degrees, but even for drummers who are fairly solid players, slight timing errors can mount into an overall sound that becomes sloppy or uneven.

Let's examine the return to a standard rock drum beat after a fill. We generally hit the crash cymbal on beat one with a solid bass drum. We will then continue playing eighth note hi-hats with the snare drum on beats two and four. But drummers will too commonly play that initial bass and crash early or late. This is often because the fill itself was either rushed or was dragging behind. The knock-on effect will then be felt until the groove is recovered—by which point the damage is done, and the drum part has ceased sounding professional.

Examine figure 3.2. This is a screenshot of the wave form from a bass drum track. The vertical line at bar 39 is exactly on beat one following a drum fill. The large white wave of sound that falls after it is the bass drum that played simultaneously with a crash cymbal to bring us back into the drumbeat following the fill. This should have been precisely on beat one, in the same place as the vertical line.

We can see that it in fact falls slightly late. The crash would probably have been late as well. The next hi-hat would possibly have been late, too, or would have had to be forced back in time, which would have made it sound rushed. If that hi-hat were not amended by beat two, the snare drum would also have been affected.

This screenshot is zoomed in significantly, and the lateness of the note is minimal. It might possibly not even make a noticeable difference to the listener. But if the note fell much later, then it would certainly have a noticeably detrimental impact on the track.

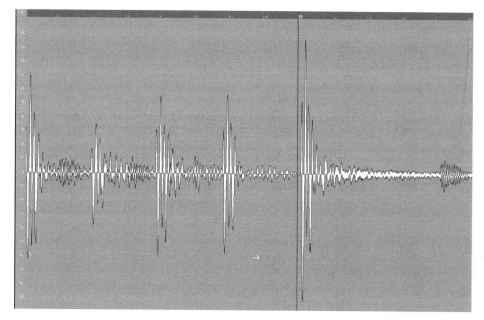

Figure 3.2.

Conversely, the same bass and crash on beat one can often be found to be early, where the drummer has rushed the fill. This is just as damaging to the rhythm. In figure 3.3 we can see the same fill and subsequent bass drum brought forward slightly. The bass drum falls slightly before the vertical line on bar 39. Now the next hi-hat and potentially the snare drum too will be rushed or, if amended, they

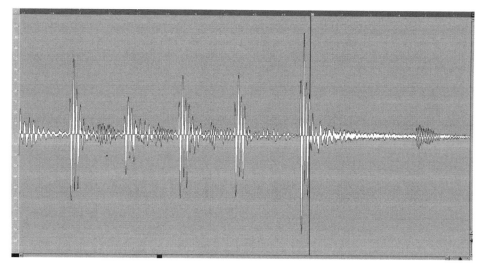

Figure 3.3.

will sound like they drag, as a space will now be created that interrupts the even eighth note flow.

Once you have identified your own timing Achilles' heel, you can use that knowledge to correct it. If you find you are always late after a fill, look at the fill itself. Are you slowing down? Use your wave form to find out, and use your ears too. Maybe the fill is perfect but you are just lazy when reaching for that crash. In which case, make a conscious effort to close that time gap until it becomes natural for you.

Taking the time to analyze your playing in this way will pay dividends thereafter as you gain a reputation for impeccable timing in everything you play.

SECRET 19: SWINGING

When the drum kit evolved, the music of the time was swung, and it was very natural for the early drummers to swing. Thanks to rock 'n' roll and drummers such as Earl Palmer, the straight eighth note hi-hat pattern developed and many of these swing drummers struggled to play straight for a while. This can be heard on some early rock 'n' roll recordings where the piano is thumping away with straight eighth notes while the drummer is still giving it a bit of swing.

Of course now much of pop and rock is straight and many modern drummers struggle to play swung rhythms. But for a working drummer that is simply not acceptable, and we must strive to develop the ability to swing no matter what our musical education has been.

When eighth notes are straight, we play perfectly even notes, all lasting for the same amount of time. When we play swung eighth notes, we are splitting a beat into a triplet (three evenly spaced notes) and then playing the first and last note of that triplet. So in effect the first note lasts for two-thirds of the beat, and the last note takes up only a third of the beat. It is this uneven nature of the two notes that creates the swing feel.

When swung eighth note drum parts are written, it is done in one of two methods. Sometimes we get the full triplets written with a number three and a bracket above to clearly state it is a triplet.

Figure 3.4.

But other times, when there are many swung notes in a piece, the part will be written with straight eighth notes and a little symbol at the start of the piece (figure 3.5). This tells us that the straight eighth notes should actually be interpreted as swung eighth notes.

Figure 3.5.

When we see this symbol, we must treat every eighth note as a swung eighth note. In which case, figure 3.6 below would sound exactly the same as figure 3.4 above.

Figure 3.6.

Learning to Swing

When learning to swing it is wise to get used to feeling the whole triplet, therefore playing three equally spaced notes in each beat. Before picking up the sticks, try counting the full triplet as below.

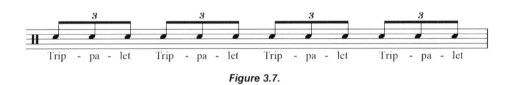

Trip - pa - let   Trip - pa - let   Trip - pa - let   Trip - pa - let

Figure 3.7.

Once you have counted, and subsequently played, this full triplet you can start to drop that middle note (the "pa"), leaving us with the swung eighth note feel. In figure 3.8 below, the "trip" lasts for two-thirds of the beat, while the "plet" lasts for only a third.

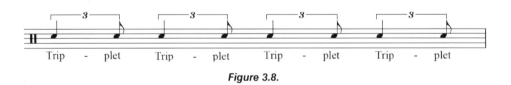

Trip - plet   Trip - plet   Trip - plet   Trip - plet

Figure 3.8.

Once this is comfortable, begin playing it as a groove. Vary the position of the bass drums and snares, play in sequence with fills (remember to play triplet-based fills), and practice along with music to really get a feel for this.

Swinging at Different Tempi

A final note on swinging is the difficulty of interpreting the appropriate feel in a range of tempi. When performing slow swing tunes, the spacing between notes is as discussed in this secret. When the music becomes much quicker, the notes are evened out so that very up-tempo jazz is actually played quite straight.

Some drummers might try to retain the full swing feel at fast speeds, but this can sound clumsy and awkward. Others may straighten out at tempos that are too slow and should still be swung, which then ruins the feel of the music.

Knowing how to swing is best learned by listening to the masters of the style. Listen to a variety of great jazz drummers such as Tony Williams, Elvin Jones, and Max Roach, to see how they temper their swing at various tempos. Try playing along and, if possible, record yourself (see Secret 3) to hear how you actually sound. By practicing this way, the ability to swing at a range of tempi will become a natural part of your playing style.

SECRET 20: ODD TIME

The comfort of our common time, also known as four/four time signature, can lead many drummers to assume that this is all they need to know for their musical career. Working within this comfort zone is inviting, and you may never feel the need to practice any other time signatures. But if you are crafting a career from music, you would be naive to adopt such an attitude.

Personally I have found myself called upon to play in numerous time signatures, both in the studio and in live situations, and I was then expected to perform them all at equally high standards.

Odd time signatures are not modern inventions. You can find them in many folk music traditions. Gaelic céilidhs involve slip jigs in nine/eight time, Filipino folk music often uses three/four time, and Balkan music features a number of challenging time signatures. In fact a drummer I know recently introduced me to Balkan music that he had played at a wedding. He later showed me a track by the Balkan Horses Band, which was in eleven/eight time.

Beyond folk, musical theater offers its own set of challenges. In this setting the music is written to support the play and therefore won't necessarily follow logical conventions of music. Frequent time signature changes occur from bar to bar, as well as tempo changes and stylistic changes. There are many jazz tracks with odd time signatures. Among the most famous examples is Dave Brubeck's "Take Five" in five/four (as well as the other tracks on his album *Time Out*) and even pop examples, such as Sting's "Seven Days" or Radiohead's "15 Step," both of which are in five/four.

The point is that odd time appears in most areas of music and isn't exclusive to progressive rock or jazz/rock fusion. If you are a working musician, at some point you will need to perform tracks in odd time at a professional standard. That means making those works *feel* great, as if you had played them your whole life, just as you would with any standard four/four pattern.

You should not assume that playing a basic pattern will suffice. You should feel comfortable playing fills, varying the patterns, moving between time signatures, reading charts simultaneously, performing difficult figures within a piece, and doing all of this with impeccable feel.

Here are some common time signatures and a basic rhythm idea within that timing. For each one, learn to play the pattern without conscious thought. Then allow yourself to improvise within that time signature: move away from and back to the rhythm; add fills; become free.

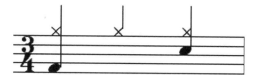

Figure 3.9.   Three/Four Time

Figure 3.10.   Six/Eight Time

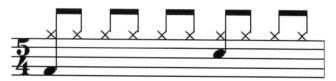

Figure 3.11.   Five/Four Time

Figure 3.12.   Seven/Eight Time

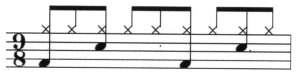

Figure 3.13.   Nine/Eight Time

If you look at the examples above, you will also find smaller phrases within some of the bars. Figure 3.11, which is in five/four, is felt as a whole bar, but figure 3.12 in seven/eight might be felt as a phrase of four and a phrase of three, with each bass drum starting the new phrase. Figure 3.13 might also be split into two phrases with each bass drum starting a phrase, forming a five-note grouping and then a four-note grouping. This can sometimes help you feel odd time signatures more naturally. You might also consider splitting less strange time signatures into irregular groups to make them sound more interesting. For example, you could split twelve/eight time into a group of five and another group of seven.

Consider other time signatures as well, and just generally make it your business to become familiar with any time signature you come across, so that next time you are called upon to step away from common time, you can do so confidently and enthusiastically.

CHAPTER 4

Accuracy Strategies

SECRET 21: LOCKED LIMBS

When we turn on any mainstream radio station, most of the songs we hear are driven by fairly basic drum patterns. These are quite often the drum beats that we learn in our early years of playing. Sometimes these grooves are adapted or embellished in such a way that they can become more challenging. But often they are not. They are just basic beats—no more, no less.

For most working drummers, most of what they play is also very basic. We might spend hours in the drum shed practicing our four-way independence, super-sonic heavy metal fills, and mathematically challenging odd time signatures. But when we actually go to work as a drummer, we generally need only a handful of simple grooves.

And yet we too often take these simple grooves for granted as beats we can all play easily and well. We don't need to practice these beats because they are so easy to play.

But you should be ready to challenge that view, as I challenged it when I once so arrogantly held it. That is because I hear too many drummers playing these simple beats who end up lacking the groove and feeling required. Sure, we can all play them, but through lack of attention, many of us play them poorly. This is one reason why top session drummers get called time and time again: they can play the simple stuff and make it feel sublime. Net result? The whole track they play on feels sublime and highly professional.

One of the main culprits for that lack of feel is the fact that the limbs are not completely locked in together. Unless a rhythm is linear, we will find certain voices of the drum kit being played together. Most often it will be a bass drum with a hi-hat, or a snare drum with a hi-hat. If these notes are not played at *exactly* the same time, a flam will occur. If this is happening throughout the song's rhythm, then the overall effect will be one of messiness and poor song quality.

So here are some exercises to help you focus on being completely locked in—being, if you will, "as one"—so that you sound in control and solid. We discussed practicing with the metronome at a slow tempo earlier. Let's return to this approach so you can have the time to really hear each note and analyze it. It is also a good idea to record these exercises for closer analysis.

Exercise 1

1. Without the metronome, play the drum beat below slowly and listen intently to every note you play. Be highly critical; correct every inaccuracy. Are the eighth note hi-hats spaced completely evenly? Is the bass drum falling completely in time with the hi-hat? Is the snare completely in time with the hi-hat?
2. Once you determine all of the above are truly locked together, set the metronome for a slow speed and repeat this exercise.
3. Once you are happy with the results, try moving into a fill and then back to the beat. Did the drum beat falter at all? Try it all again.

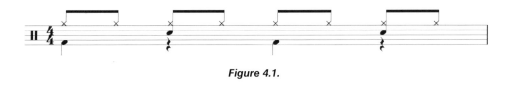

Figure 4.1.

Exercise 2

In figure 4.2, we have the same beat, except we have added bass drums on beats two and four, which is a very common rhythm. The challenge here is that three limbs are now playing simultaneously on beats two and four. These still need to retain that accuracy so that we hear one big, weighty note, rather than three thin, messy notes. Getting those notes locked in together makes the difference between a messy rhythm and a very powerful, effective rhythm.

Repeat the three steps from Exercise 1 with this drum beat.

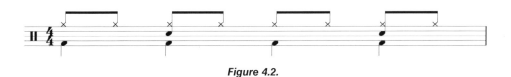

Figure 4.2.

Exercise 3

In figure 4.3, we take things up a notch by adding sixteenth note hi-hats. This creates the classic disco feel that omits the hi-hat from beats two and four because the hand pattern is played as a single stroke roll. Even though you only have the right-handed snare and bass drum to lock in on those beats, you now have twice as many hi-hats to keep even and the hand-to-hand aspect, which can cause their own problems.

Again, repeat the three steps and listen vigilantly for any imperfections.

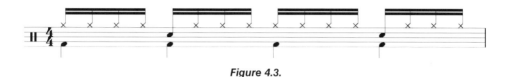

Figure 4.3.

SECRET 22: SPEED BURSTS

When trying to develop the speed of a certain exercise or musical passage, the accuracy can suffer as the focus turns to pushing the tempo up. It is easy to allow the quality of the sound you produce to become lost as speed takes precedence over accuracy. The technique when striking the drum, the tone achieved from the drum, and the even timing between notes can all too easily suffer if we are not attentive. You must consider the quality of sound and timing at every stage of the process when building the speed.

One popular method to build speed is to gradually increase the tempo, week by week, day by day. By notching it up gradually—for example in five-bpm increments—we acclimatize to each small increase before moving up the speed once more.

But sometimes you might need to reach a specific speed by a specific date in the not-too-distant future and you just haven't the luxury of time to get there at the rate of five bpm a week. In this situation, speed bursts might help. This technique can help build speed while maintaining accuracy. We will use the single stroke roll to keep things simple. This method involves playing at a tempo that is very comfortable, but then doubling the speed for several short notes, creating that burst of speed. We will then return to our safe tempo before the pattern has collapsed. By repeating this short burst of speed, you gradually get used to the pattern at that sped-up pace. You can then increase the lengths of the bursts until, eventually, you can maintain that speed indefinitely.

In figure 4.4, the exercises below show a sixteenth note single stroke roll, which doubles in speed to thirty-second notes (demi-semi-quavers) for short bursts. Start the sixteenth notes at a speed you feel very comfortable with *and* that you can just about double for a short burst (so, for example, at 100 bpm if your original speed was 50 bpm).

Set the metronome and play the first line, keeping to a single stroke roll sticking. Repeat this first line for as long as you need to become comfortable.

Now move to line two. Here the thirty second notes last for twice as long. Again, repeat this line until comfortable. Now move through line three and beyond with the same process.

If at any point you physically cannot move to the next line and maintain the quality of your playing, take a rest. Come back and start from the beginning after ten minutes. You might need to resume in a day or a week. It doesn't matter as long as you never lose the quality of the sound you produce. By the end of this process you should be able to play the whole bar as thirty second notes with total accuracy, having thus effectively doubled your speed.

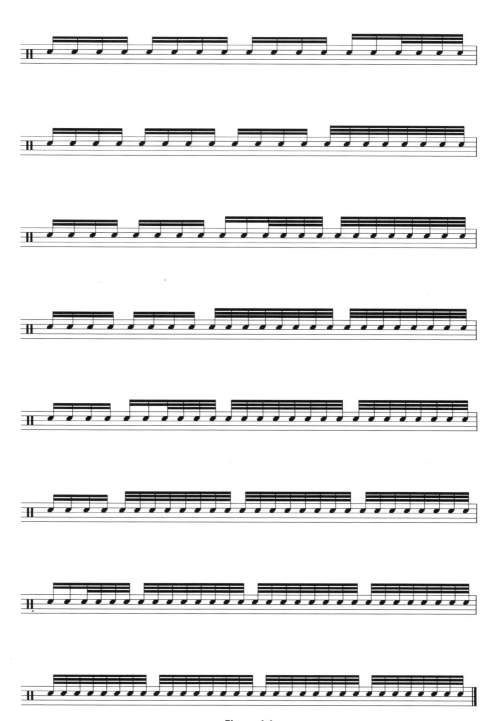

Figure 4.4.

CHAPTER 5

Equipment Strategies

SECRET 23: CHOOSING DRUMS

Unless you are in a fortunate financial position, choosing your drums will be a very important decision in your career that you will want to get right. Everything that you are as a drummer will be reflected through your drum kit. Even if you are the most technically gifted drummer in the world, if your drums don't sound good, you will not sound good.

Make no mistake: good drums are expensive. Thorough research is thus necessary before committing to your kit and its components. Over time, you might build a collection of drums from which you can choose what is most appropriate for each situation. But many still have to make do with one kit.

There are a number of considerations when choosing your drums, and we will discuss them individually.

Genre

Possibly the most important decision-making factor is genre. You've probably noticed that Joey Jordison owned a different drum kit from Elvin Jones. This is obvious to most of us, as their instruments were required to create very different sounds. So identifying what you need to get out of your drums should be your first thought when selecting a kit.

Many drummers playing older styles, such as jazz, soul, or funk, look for a traditional sound from their kit. Vintage drums, such as round badge Gretsch kits, are very popular. For a more modern example, kits like Yamaha's Club Custom range also represent a good choice since they are designed to retain the qualities of the older kits through the adjustment of modern manufacturing techniques. On the other hand, drummers playing contemporary styles will often choose the most cutting-edge drums for that fresh look and modern sound.

Size

Genre can also dictate component size. A jazz drummer might choose an 18-inch bass drum, then 12- and 14-inch toms. A heavy rock drummer would certainly require a larger 22-inch (or higher) bass drum and much bigger toms, such as the standard rock sizes of 12, 13, and 16 inches. If you wanted a slightly tighter sound, you may opt for fusion sizes with a 20-inch bass drum and then 10-, 12-, and 14-inch toms.

But you shouldn't only consider diameter. Depths also change with other sonic fashions, such as the power toms of the 1980s, which were heavily sought given their extra one inch of depth. There are square toms, with an equal depth to diameter, and shallow toms, such as Tama's Hyperdrive, with its much bigger diameter-to-depth ratio. Will you want the fast attack and quick decay of Hyperdrive toms or the longer note of the deeper toms?

Drilled or Not

The traditional method for attaching toms to a bass drum was to drill a big hole in the side of each tom and another in the top of the bass drum, then attach them with metal tubing. By the 1980s, drummers thought this drilling seriously impeded the drum's natural resonance and so various mounting systems were marketed by major drum manufacturers such as Yamaha's YESS system or Pearl's ISS system. As a result, the bass drum stayed intact while the toms escaped drilling. Various clever mounts avoided metal-on-metal contact and were attached to the tension rods or rims of the tom. These mounts then clamped to cymbal stands or rack systems. Now the drum could resonate freely. This arrangement also allowed for greater positioning since the toms were no longer stuck atop the bass drum.

Whether you select this type of kit is entirely up to you. Many professionals such as Steve Gadd still play with toms attached to bass drums, so the arrangement is not nearly as universal as you might think.

Material

Today there are so many options for shell material, with maple, birch, beech, mahogany, oak, poplar, and basswood dominating catalog offerings. At the top end of the big manufacturers' lines, you can also custom design your drums by mixing and matching woods.

Personal opinions on this subject are legion, but you should know that there is no right or wrong. Birch and maple are the two most popular woods, and there is a clear difference in their fundamental tones. Maple produces a rounder, more sustained sound, with even highs and mids, and offers more low frequencies.

Meanwhile birch produces a more controlled, focused sound, with boosted high frequencies and good low-end frequencies, but fewer mids. Maple has thus become a good choice for live drums while birch has become a standard for recording drums, such as the Yamaha Recording Custom or Pearl Custom Studio.

You will also notice that drums come in a wide variety of plies. This can also confuse buyers as each manufacturer potentially uses different thicknesses of wood for each ply, so that a 15-ply DW drum might actually be thinner than a 10-ply Yamaha drum. When considering the thickness of your drum, bear in mind that a thinner drum will vibrate more easily, transferring energy from the head to the shell to create a rich "woody" tone. This is best appreciated by near-field applications such as recording. Thicker shells are very efficient and allow more of the sound to be projected to the audience, making them louder and thus better suited to live and noisy environments.

Number of Drums

The number of drums you use will vary from gig to gig. But one thing that comes with experience is the realization that it is not wise to bring anything that you won't need. Carrying extra equipment, tuning it, setting it up, and getting comfortable behind it are all critical, albeit time-consuming, tasks, which you should therefore keep to the necessary minimum. If you only need two toms to play the set, don't set up seven of them. This issue becomes even more important when recording since extra microphones increase phase issues and mixing problems.

However, when buying drums, you may want to buy a larger set so you can have more options. I commonly change my kit to fit the gig. That might mean a smaller bass drum or extra toms or fewer toms and a unique mix of snares and so on.

Try to think about what you need from your kit in the present and also what you think you might need from it in the future.

Die Cast or Triple Flanged

Triple flanged hoops are bent into shape while die cast hoops are formed in a die. Triple flanged hoops are easier to tune because they are more forgiving and flexible while die cast take more precision to perfectly tune. Triple flanged hoops can make the drum seem softer when you hit it, whereas die cast hoops are very rigid and make the drum response sound harder. Once again, your selection is a question of personal choice, but if you're looking for a cracking backbeat from your snare drum, then you would go for die cast hoops on just that drum, with perhaps warmer triple flanged hoops on your toms.

Heads

Heads are a hugely important aspect of your drum sound and are discussed in Secret 26.

What's important here is that all drummers are still just people who respond to the different qualities in a drum. Think about your musical applications, yes, but also follow your heart and choose an instrument that excites you. That is the instrument that will bring out the best in your playing.

SECRET 24: CHOOSING CYMBALS

There are more varieties of cymbal today than there have ever been. The categories of crashes, rides, hi-hats, splashes, chinas, and other effects cymbals serve as pigeonholes within which all manner of the weird and wonderful can go on display. The sheer number of available choices can daunt the most experienced of drummers, especially as they come face to face with the prospect of parting with large sums of money. Choose the wrong cymbals and the music will suffer as the other musicians around you grow frustrated, you lose passion for the sound you're generating, and the cymbals themselves even break.

As in the selection of drums, when choosing cymbals, first ascertain what you need them to do. The genre, other instruments, venue size, and your own playing style are all key determinants.

If you are playing acoustic jazz in a small club, your musical requirements will differ from a drummer who is on stage for a heavy metal gig in a stadium. The ride cymbal needed to cut through distorted guitars at high volume and reach the back of a football field will differ significantly from that needed to keep swinging with an upright acoustic bass without drowning it out.

But even in the same-sized room, heavy distorted guitars may require cymbals that cut through while in other scenarios you need to find cymbals that won't dominate. Even in the same genre, the size of the venue will have an impact. For a club, a 16-inch crash might suffice, whereas an arena might well require larger crashes to create a big enough sound. (Note that this is not the same as mere "volume," since the arena sound systems will obviously pick up and project the sound of the cymbals.)

Construction

Cymbals are either formed from sheet metal or cast. The traditional casting method involves pouring molten metal into a cast, then a sequence of cooling, sorting, heating, rolling, shaping, hammering, and lathing follow to create the required shape and sound. These cymbals achieve great clarity and durability and create a full, rich tone. Many see the sound of cast cymbals as improving with age, which explains the high prices for vintage cymbals.

Sheet cymbals are cut from pre-formed discs of metal to exactly fit the required series for which they are intended. They are then hammered to create the required tone. These cymbals often have a faster response but also a faster decay time. They also often live at the cheaper end of a manufacturer's product list.

Weight

Cymbals come in many different weights and how hard you hit the cymbal might determine your choice. Thin cymbals will crack quickly if you play hard. To that end, models like Zildjian Z offer a thicker option to save on the cost of replacing light K cymbals. Thinner cymbals produce sound more quickly and with less volume than thicker cymbals. Select these then for lighter situations or recording studios, where excessive volume is not required. Note that the thickness also affects the pitch of the cymbal.

In fact, several aspects affect pitch from the curvature (flatter cymbals produce a lower pitch) to the size (larger cymbals create a higher pitch) to the thickness (thicker cymbals have a higher pitch).

The bell of a cymbal also has a significant bearing on the sound (beyond that of simply hitting the bell itself). If the cymbal bell is small, it will create a drier sound. If the bell is large, the cymbal will sound livelier.

As a general rule of thumb, the darker cymbals, such as Zildjian's K Custom Dark, will suit jazzier applications, while brighter cymbals, such as Zildjian's A Custom, would suit more contemporary styles. There is no substitute for trying cymbals before you buy them, and you should always trust your own ears. Media reviews, artists associations, and online sound samples are all useful, but listen to the cymbal being played in the same room and follow your instinct. Your cymbal sound will be a big part of the sound you create as a drummer, so take the time to make these choices for yourself.

Ideally, as a professional musician you should aim to have a strong selection of cymbals so you can cover each situation that arises with the appropriate cymbal. Over time you should look to develop your collection and understand the strength of each cymbal you own.

SECRET 25: CHOOSING DRUMSTICKS

Walking into a well-stocked music shop to purchase a pair of drumsticks may cause you to stop dead in your tracks as you face that wall of pigeonholes, each stacked with a variety of items with which to hit drums.

First there is the choice of materials. Some of the popular woods include rosewood, which is a very dense and hard wood; maple, which is light and soft; hickory, which is slightly harder and more durable than maple; and Japanese oak, which is very hard, durable, and heavy. Beyond wood, a drummer may also consider carbon fiber, graphite, aluminium, fiber glass, plastic, sticks with LEDs that illuminate upon impact, or ergonomic sticks that fit the contours of the hand. There is also the market of signature sticks that just about every well-known drummer in the professional arena has designed to his or her personal specifications. Most just offer an alternative size, weight, or balance, but there are some more unusual sticks on offer.

Each stick consists of the same basic design features. These comprise the butt (bottom end), shaft (straight area, which the hand grips), shoulder (tapered area), and tip (which strikes the drumhead). The tapered area could be very gradual on a lighter drumstick or very severe on a heavier stick.

Furthermore, since 1958, thanks to Joe Calato of the American drumstick company Regal Tip, we have the nylon tip. In response to the damage caused to the tips of wooden drumsticks, Calato designed a nylon tip to protect the tip while also achieving a brighter, more articulate sound. The wood tip, on the other hand, offers a warmer, more organic sound.

Beyond the bright-sounding nylon tip, the timbre can dramatically change depending on the tip of the stick. Many different shapes and sizes are offered in the market, but the popular types are a round tip, olive tip, barrel tip, or pointed tip. The round tip is bright and focused; the olive tip offers full, low tones and increased durability; and while the barrel and pointed tips both offer a medium tone, the barrel has more focus owing to its decreased contact area.

So Which Stick Do You Choose?

Luckily a universally recognized numbering system was devised in the 20th century to help drummers. Although different manufacturers vary the sizing slightly, this system does provide a rough guide as to what we should buy. In this system a letter and a number are assigned to the sticks. The letter refers to the intended application of the stick as denoted by S, A, and B. The A confusingly stands for orchestra. These sticks are the lightest and were initially intended for big band group playing. The B stands for band, with the original application of brass bands and symphonic concert bands. These were heavier than the A sticks but still able to play at softer dynamics. The third letter, S, stands for street and were designed as the largest and heaviest available. Street uses include marching band and drum corps. The accompanying number refers to the circumference of the stick, with the larger the number, the smaller the circumference. The most popular numbers are 5, 7, and 2.

Although bearing the A for orchestra in the original plan, 5A is a very popular choice as the standard stick for drum kit applications. This choice is a sensible place to start for most players. For younger drummers who require a lighter stick, 7A is a great alternative. If you're a large individual and want to hit hard, try a 5B or even a 2B. Beyond these standard sizes, specialist sticks are now manufactured for more specific uses. So we have everything from heavy metal sticks, which are of course larger than lighter jazz sticks—and everything in between. Some heavy players also use metal sticks made by companies such as Ahead and promoted by such players as Metallica's Lars Ulrich or Slipknot's Joey Jordison. These are very durable but don't have anywhere near the feel of wooden sticks and inhibit the effectiveness of certain techniques, such as cross sticks.

With respect to wood type, nylon vs. wood tip, and much else, what you select is a personal decision. There are no right or wrong selections per se, and it may take years of experimentation before you find what works best for you. Obviously, you should visit your local music shop, pick up different sizes, and get a feel for them. If they feel good, that's more than likely a good start.

Drummers who are especially meticulous will roll the sticks on a flat surface at the shop to detect imperfections that may cause "bananas" (bends in the stick). Even more meticulous drummers will tap the sticks in a way to ascertain the fundamental tone of the stick itself, ensuring that each stick is the same and that the notes played by them will sound even. But with modern manufacturing processes, top brands tend to be very consistent in providing matched sticks, so that such testing techniques may be superfluous (although there is no harm in learning them).

Finally, the professionally oriented drummer should have enough selections in their stick bag to cover a broad range of scenarios. This is discussed in detail in Secret 29: Essential Equipment.

SECRET 26: TUNING—THE BLACK ART

Many consider tuning a drum to be something of a black art. Others see it as unimportant. After all, most drummers don't tune to a specific pitch, as a violinist or guitarist would. As long as it makes a sound like a drum, then that's good enough. Historically many professional drummers held this view until close microphone techniques placed the individual drums under the acoustic microscope, and drummers had to adapt to please sound engineers.

Often this added scrutiny took the route of deadening the drum with cigarette packets, wallets, gaffa tape, and anything else on hand. The problem with this approach is that of choking the sound of this wonderful instrument, squeezing its tone and character down until we are left with an instrument that might as well be a cardboard box.

Too many drummers with expensive kits fail to tune properly. As a result, their instrument sounds dire, in contrast to mid-range kits that sound well beyond their price range because they were properly tuned.

Many a drummer has let it be known that he needs a new snare, or even entire drum kit, when upon inspection of their allegedly inadequate kit, it is clear that what is needed is good old-fashioned tuning of the existing heads. Once they're tuned, it's no surprise to find the drum kit owner excited by his rejuvenated drum set, which suddenly sounds new again.

Heads

If anything does need replacing, it is generally the drum head rather than the drum itself. Heads can reach a point where they can no longer be tuned, something that will happen more quickly if you're a hard hitter.

When selecting heads, there are many from which to choose. As a general rule, thinner heads resonate more freely and offer more tone. These are better for recording and include the likes of Evans G1, Remo Diplomat, or Remo Ambassador. If you are a light player, or are performing a lighter style such as jazz, look for these.

Thicker heads offer more durability, so if you're practicing at home or performing rock gigs and can't afford to keep replacing your split Ambassadors, try these on. For recording, however, thicker heads lack the tone and vibrancy of their thinner counterparts. If you do go with a thicker head, options include the Evans G2, Evans EC2, and Remo Pinstripe.

The bottom head is known as the resonant head. To allow it to resonate, it is much thinner. Such heads as Remo Diplomats are great for toms. As for the snare drum, some drummers use batter heads on the bottom but many will use the purpose-made resonant heads offered by all the top brands such as the Remo Diplomat Hazy Snare side.

Tuning

Before putting the new head on, make sure you have cleaned the debris and dust from the inside of the shell and around the bearing edges. Check that the bearing edges are in good condition as any imperfections will result in impossible tuning. If they are damaged, find a music shop that will recut them.

1. Place the head on your drum, place the rim on the head, and slot the tension rods down into the lugs. Some drummers lubricate the tension rods with Vaseline.
2. Tighten each tension rod with your fingers. Always move across the drum and never to the tension rod next to where you started. If you begin at the 12 o'clock position, the next tension rod to be tuned is the one at 6 o'clock. Next you do the one at 1 o'clock, then 7 o'clock, and so on. This allows the tension to be spread evenly around the drum.

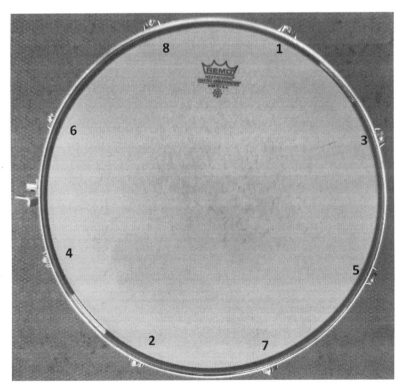

Figure 5.1.

3. It will still be quite loose at this stage and wrinkles should be present. If it is a new head, you will want to seat the drumhead. Place one hand on the center of the drum palm down. Place the other hand over it as if giving CPR. Push down fairly hard until you hear a terrifying splitting sound. Now relax: you haven't broken the head. You've just broken it in, allowing the bond between the glue and the rim to stretch to the shape of the drum.

4. Now, using the drum key start back at 12 o'clock and turn it 180 degrees. Now go around the drum, crisscrossing again with the half turn on each tension rod.

5. Repeat step 3 until the drum is close to the pitch that you want. You will want to apply much smaller increments when it is close to the desired sound. Consider a 90-degree or 45-degree turn on each tension rod.

Fine-Tuning

We are now close to being fully tuned, but there is one more stage. To fine-tune the drum you must tap the head an inch in from each tension rod. The pitch should be identical on each. That means the drum is evenly tuned. If one area is different in pitch, tweak it with the drum key and use your ear to listen until each part of the drum sounds even.

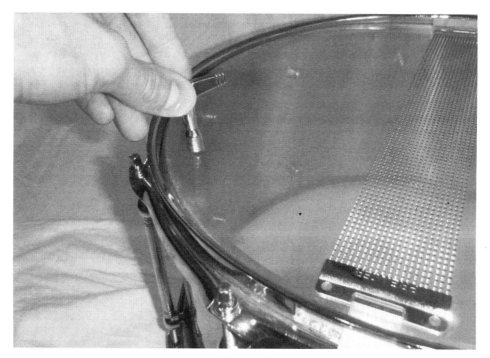

Figure 5.2.

Snare Drum

Generally considered the most important drum of the drum kit, it is also very personal. Listen to ten great drummers and you will hear ten different snare sounds. The sound is affected by the snare drum shell material, snare heads, bearing edges, tuning, snare strand tension, playing style, and so on. You must find the right head combination and tuning for your own playing and application.

Often drummers try to eliminate the dreaded ringing from the snare, but this area should be approached with caution. Although excessive ringing is offensive and detrimental to your sound, if you completely eliminate it, the drum will sound choked and boxy.

When tuning the snare drum, take the snare off so you can truly hear the drumhead without the distracting buzzes. One method to get these out of the way is to turn the drum upside down and carefully slide a stick beneath the wires so that it is left resting on the rim with the snare stretched over the top and away from the resonant head.

Figure 5.3.

If you are fitting a new head, you will have to remove the snares completely. When tuning this resonant head, use the discussed tuning method (without the need to seat it because it is very thin) but take this head up higher than any other. This is the tightest head on the drum kit, but always use your ears and be careful not to overtighten. You should next tune the batter head. This will generally be tuned lower in pitch than the resonant head, but tension between different drummers' snare drum batter heads varies dramatically. Ultimately this is down to personal taste, but you could start with trying it a third lower. To hear the individual heads pitch, mute one head with your hand and play the opposite head. Then reverse this to hear the other head. Due to the advanced techniques often applied to this head, you will need to find the right balance between sound and feel. When you reapply the snare wires, you may find that they excessively buzz. Read Secret 27: Eliminating Snare Buzz for some solutions. Also read Secret 28: Getting the Right Snare Sound for Each Song to learn some general rules for different styles and applications.

Toms

These require the same tuning technique as above, but the relationships between the toms are important here. Many drummers tune toms a fourth apart. You can use a piano to get an idea of how this interval sounds. Some drummers are very specific and tune to exact pitches whereas others are happy with the approximate sound of the fourth. At the piano, hit a C note. Then go down and hit a G and then finally the D. That is the sound you want to aim for between three toms.

The relationship between the resonant and batter head is also important and, again, down to personal preference. As a general rule, the batter head primarily affects the tone, while the resonant head affects the note length. If the batter head is tensioned differently to the resonant head, it will decrease the resonance but may cause a pitch bend effect in the note sustain, which can be undesirable. Tuned to the same tension the resonance might be too long. It's a case of trial and error to find your preference.

The choice of heads in relation to each other is also worth carefully considering. You may wish to use a batter head and resonant head of equal thickness. A double-ply batter might not react accordingly with a thin single-ply resonant head so you could consider a heavier resonant head.

The resonant head really is crucial to your tom sound so begin with this drum when tuning. Having taken it through the tuning process, you must now use your ears to fine-tune. We are looking for the drum to really sing, by creating a very pleasing tone. It is imperative that the note is even, with a smooth decay. To achieve this, take great care with the fine-tuning stage. Many drums will have a natural pitch at which they sing in the most pleasing manner. You have to be realistic here; an 8-inch tom will have a very particular pitch range at which it works so don't try to make it sound like a 12-inch tom.

Bass Drum

In many styles, the bass drum is the easiest to tune as we drummers tend to muffle it to get a dull thud sound. Some drummers simply finger tighten each lug so that the wrinkles are only just taken out. Some use the drum key and go much tighter. Regarding muffling, some heads such as the Evans E-mad have their own integrated muffling systems. However, often something is placed inside the drum to achieve that dead sound depending on how much boom each drummer wishes to retain.

This might be a pillow, a towel, an EQ cushion (which is in essence a more expensive pillow sold by drumhead manufacturers), or a dead body (just testing if you are concentrating!). Play around and see what works for you in your particular setting. It is important to remember that each concert hall will create a very different sound for your kit. You must treat each venue differently and be prepared to adapt your sound to work in each environment.

To Tape or Not to Tape?

Over the years many different materials have been placed upon drums to achieve certain sounds. These range from gaffa tape to paper towels, wallets, cigarette packets, tea towels, and anything else that does the job. Purpose-made solutions include the O-rings and Moongel, both of which should be part of any drummer's toolbox to help control unwanted overtones if and when they arise in different studios or concert halls. Moongel is a very versatile product as the placement of the gel changes the severity of the dampening. It is also very easy to use more than one piece or even cut a single piece down if you desire less dampening.

My opinion is that you shouldn't get caught thinking that the use of such techniques indicates your inadequacy to tune a drum. If it helps achieve the best sound, which ultimately helps you to offer the best drum track that the artist, producer, or client is looking for, then do it. Every room causes the drum to react differently and your combination of drums and heads might just need a little helping hand for certain styles in certain situations. Do what you can to get a great sound.

Learning to tune your instrument is vital, and not something you can ignore. However, there are products on the market to help you tune. These should not be used to be lazy and avoid learning to tune drums. But in some situations they can be a great help.

Figure 5.4.   Moongel

Figure 5.5.   Drumdial. Courtesy of Drumdial

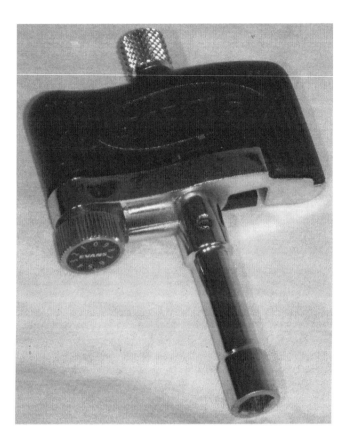

Figure 5.6.   Evans Torque Key

Such products include the Tama Tension Watch, the DrumDial, and the Evans Torque Key. These all provide us with an accurate way to reach a specific tension on each tension rod without having to hit the drum at all.

I use a torque key occasionally when the on-stage noise from guitarists who find it necessary to tune their instrument at top volume prevents me from hearing my drums, or mid-performance when there is little time for, or tolerance of, a noisy and lengthy drum tune. This allows me to very quickly tighten a loosened tension rod to a set tension, and without even hitting it I know it is at the required tension.

SECRET 27: ELIMINATING SNARE BUZZ

Drum kits sometimes appear like living, breathing creatures, working as one beast with each limb having an effect on the others. These seemingly uncontrollable components resonate and ring together, making it difficult to tame. This is part of what creates the individual character and allure of each kit, but it can also lead to problems that need controlling. One such common problem is the excessive buzzing of the snare wires.

When approaching snare buzz, there are a couple of things to determine. Firstly, what is causing this offense to occur? Is it your high tom? Is it a particular note that the bass player is playing? Is it every possible sound in the room?

The second consideration is whether this is actually a problem. After all, it is part of the sound of the drum and if we take away all of the drum kit's characteristics, we are left with a lifeless instrument. So the trick here is to really help control the sound, which might require slightly different actions in each situation.

If you are performing an intimate gig on a small stage, with the bass player right beside you, then you might find that particular frequencies that he plays send your snare's wires into a buzzing frenzy. This sympathetic buzz can cause big problems in certain situations. If the gig is a noisy rock show, these buzzing sounds will most likely get lost in the wall of sound that the whole band produces. If this is an acoustic gig with a wonderful singer and sweet string parts, then the buzzes will be very exposed and will soon start to annoy musicians on stage and audience members alike.

If the drummer is in an isolated recording studio booth, or barricaded on a stage by Perspex, then you might find that the sympathetic buzz is no longer a problem and you can enjoy the personality of your snare drum without consequence.

However, sometimes the sympathetic buzz comes from closer to home and the offender is your high tom. This tom sits directly in front of the snare so any issues here will be hard to avoid due to proximity. The problem lies within frequencies that respond to each other, usually as a result of being too close in pitch. The only way to alleviate this is to tune the tom or snare to another pitch. Of course, if re-tuning the high tom, you will then have to check the relative tuning of the other toms to make sure they still sound good together. And you may have also taken the tom away from its fundamental pitch now, so it will be difficult to make it sound as good.

Before you start detuning toms, you might want to try a little trick with the snare drum itself. Although we have spent a long time tuning our drums so that every tension rod gives identical tension, we could break this rule for the snare drum's resonant head. Here we can loosen the tension rod on either side of the snare wires, on both ends of the snare wire strand.

Figure 5.7.

To compensate for this loss of tension, you will then need to tighten the remaining tension rods to achieve the required sound and feel when playing the drum. This is often enough to remove undesired buzz but still retain all the qualities we want in a snare drum.

It may also be worth considering different head and snare wire combinations. You may be using heads that are incredibly thin and unsuitable for your particular style or type of performance. Furthermore, products such as Puresound's Equalizer snare wires are designed to help reduce sympathetic vibrations. Beyond that, an old solution is to place felt, tape, or Moongel under or across the ends of the snare wires. When utilizing any such approach, do so with caution as there is often an adverse effect on the sound of your drum.

SECRET 28: GETTING THE RIGHT SNARE SOUND FOR EACH SONG

Snare sounds come in such great variety from very resonant, ringy sounds to very dead sounds; from incredibly loud to very soft and sensitive; from high-pitched cracks to deep and full thuds. There are nearly as many snare sounds as there are drummers.

The snare drum is often considered the most important part of the drum kit. For many, this is their identity. The toms and bass are important, but a snare drum sound can make or break a track. Some drummers become well known for a particular snare drum sound, while others will have many sounds to cope with the great demand of their varied musical work.

You may like to build a collection of snare drums that have particular tuning ranges or other sonic strengths to fulfill particular roles. But often a single drum, such as the Ludwig 400, will be very versatile and offer many possibilities through different tuning and muffling options.

Below are some general guidelines for generic sounds in some popular styles.

Rock

Within such a wide genre, many different snares will be found among the various subgenres of rock. But in general, the style is loud and powerful, and therefore a drum will need to cope with this. Greater depths such as six or seven inches will be found here, and specific heads are designed for such playing. Remo's Emperor X heads are one such example. These feature two 10-millimeter heads with an added 5-millimeter center dot beneath the main heads. Lower tunings may offer a fatter sound, though a tighter crack may be desired to cut through the wall of sound with the added depth of the drum providing the weight needed. Snare tension depends on personal taste and application.

Funk

One of the most celebrated funk players is David Garibaldi of Tower of Power. He achieves a great sound for funk based around a tight snare modeled on the high-pitched sound of his signature 3.5-inch deep piccolo snare. He tensions both heads very tightly to achieve a cutting "crack" sound. He then adjusts the snare strainer to the point that even when playing light ghost notes, the snares are still excited enough to hear them but not too loose that they are rattling uncontrollably. He then loosens one or two tension rods of the drum to add an element of depth to that tight sound. Finally, he uses a small square of Moongel on the batter head.

R&B/Hip-Hop

This style often necessitates a very tight snare sound, frequently attempting to re-create an album sound that may have been produced electronically. This can be achieved with a tight tuning and minimal snare buzz. Smaller snare diameters such as 13 inches might also be preferable.

Drum and Bass

The history of this style is discussed in *The Drum: A History*, published by Scarecrow Press. Here you will see that drum and bass and jungle developed from the great funk drummers of the 1960s. When these original recordings were sped up, the pitch of the snare was raised with it. Therefore, a tight tuning is required upon a shallow snare drum. Specific drums are now marketed, such as Sonor's Select Jungle Snare. This example has a depth of two inches and features 16 jingles cut into the drum shell to obtain an authentic sound. They also produce an entire drum kit in this range to cover playing this style.

Jazz

The snare drums marketed as jazz snare drums are often a medium depth and 14-inch diameter, although great jazz players such as Jeff "Tain" Watts often use deeper drums such as his 6.5-inch deep snare on the Branford Marsalis *A Love Supreme* DVD recording. Generally this style requires lighter playing and therefore greater response from the heads. Thinner resonant heads and specifically designed batter heads such as Remo's Fibreskyn might be worth considering. If you will be using brushes, you will also need a good coated head to achieve the appropriate friction.

Reggae

A great example of a reggae sound is that of Carlton Barrett with Bob Marley and the Wailers. His distinctive sound is now synonymous with reggae, and he achieved this by disengaging the strainer on his drum and tuning the heads very tight, obtaining an almost timbale type sound. You will certainly want a sound that works well with the cross-stick technique and the ability to play timbale-esque rim shots during fills.

Blues

Blues players will often look for an authentic vintage sound. Looser tunings are often found here as well as looser snare strainers for a full and fat buzzing sound, although not so loose that it can't handle the lower dynamics. An open sound rather than overly muffled is often sought after, but again, great variety will be found with many great players contradicting this. Of course, a funky blues setting might require a tighter sound, and a small club blues setting might require brushes so a very sensitive snare might be required. As with all genres, achieve the right snare sound for each particular setting.

SECRET 29: ESSENTIAL EQUIPMENT

As drummers we have a pretty bad deal when it comes to transporting equipment to a performance. The large and multi-itemed nature of our instrument usually necessitates a car, city road tolls, parking, terrible traffic, and so on. Meanwhile our harmonica-playing friends jump on a train with their instrument in their pocket and turn up at the venue ready to play within minutes. But that was our choice so we must avoid grumbling.

Fortunately many musical scenarios allow for a drum kit to be provided, whether it's a hire kit from an external company or a house kit at the venue. These kits will be found in a range of conditions from the perfectly tuned and maintained right down to the practically unplayable and everything in between.

As professionally minded musicians, we must be able to do our job on whatever we are presented with, and do so without fuss. This can be difficult when the toms sound like cardboard boxes, the stool is so wobbly that you have trouble using your feet on the pedals, the cymbal stands are without washers and wingnuts, and the hi-hat stand barely lifts the hi-hat when you press the pedal.

Even if we are using great equipment that we are familiar with, we will find each room and each playing situation will present different requirements in terms of tuning and dampening that we must meet.

Some of these difficulties are impossible to overcome, but others are quite easy to circumvent if we are prepared for all possibilities. As the old adage goes, "Fail to prepare and you prepare to fail."

So here is a list of essential items that allow you to be prepared for whatever equipment and sound difficulties with which you are faced. Whether using your own equipment or a hire kit, always ensure you arrive with these items in your stick bag.

1. **Drumsticks**. Obvious I know, but it is wise to keep a variety of sticks to cater for any situation. Keep a range of sizes and weights so you have some heavier sticks for rock, light sticks for jazz, as well as wood tips and nylon tips for different sounds (see Secret 25). For different applications, you should also have some hot rods, brushes, and mallets.

2. **Drum key**. Never be without this. You need to be able to keep your drums well tuned and appropriately tuned for each room and playing style. The drums will also detune as you play them, so regular retuning might be necessary. If it is a hire kit, the chance that it is tuned just right for you is slim, so be ready to tune these as soon as you arrive. I also like to keep a torque key, like that produced by Evans, so that I can adjust a detuned drum mid-set without wasting time or banging around (see Secret 26).

3. **Gaffa tape/Moongel**. Some kind of strong tape is very useful for many applications. It is a long-standing method for dampening the rebellious drum with excessive overtones, although this might be better treated with accurate tuning. But it is also great for holding things together that are falling apart, taping things down that we want to stay where they are, and a whole lot more. If using tape for drum sound improvement, we may prefer to use products such as Moongel that are specifically designed for this purpose and are very adaptable.

4. **Ear plugs**. Although these might distract us or impair our enjoyment of live music, we must take the risk to our hearing seriously. If we damage our hearing, then we will no longer enjoy music at all. See Secret 31 for a detailed discussion of this. Be sure to keep some in your stick bag at all times.

5. **Metronome.** You will most likely be the band member responsible for counting off a majority of the songs. Even if you have no intention of playing along with the click at a gig, it is a very useful tool to have as a reference when starting a song. If you count off at the wrong speed, the entire song could be a disaster. The advent of apps means that you can even use your smart phone to provide this.

6. **Spare snare.** If a tom head breaks or the drum is damaged somehow, you will still be able to limp through the set, and depending on the material of the show and how many other toms you have, possibly no one will notice any difference. But if you damage a snare drum, you will most likely find that you cannot play a single track from the set. It would be a disaster. So be prepared. At the very least, take a spare snare head. If space allows it, just pack a second snare. I also like to take a second bass drum batter head because this drum is also integral to most drum patterns. A second bass drum is impractical, but the spare head doesn't cause me any problems to pack.

7. **Felts, Washers, etc.** As mentioned, many hire kits are in a poor state and you will not want to place your expensive cymbals on a cymbal stand that is without felts or plastic tubing. Keep a pocket of your stick bag for spare felts, cymbal-protecting plastic tubing, wingnuts, tension rods, spare drum keys, and washers. Just remember to pack them back in your stick bag at the end.

8. **Manuscript paper and pencil.** Often I am called upon to learn a set for a gig in a couple of days. Or I'm at a rehearsal and parts are suddenly changed just before a show. Sometimes there just isn't the chance to fully commit every note to memory, so writing parts down is essential. You might also find yourself in a moment of inspiration and want to record your creation somehow. A handy manuscript pad makes all this easy.

SECRET 30: EMBRACING TECHNOLOGY

We drummers are largely an old-fashioned bunch at heart. We play one of the world's oldest instruments, and we enjoy that earthy connection with the wood and animal skin that resonates when we beat it. The idea of circuit boards and wires seems far removed from what attracted us to the drum initially, and although the available technology improves every year, it will surely never match the nuances and character of an acoustic drum.

However, as a drummer wishing to make a career from music, it would be foolhardy to ignore the significance of technology in music. The increased use of technology in music equates to an increased demand for drummers to use such technology both live and in the studio. If you do not keep pace with this use, you may lose out on a gig to someone who is au fait with the equipment.

At the time of writing, British singer Robbie Williams had just completed a large tour. His drummer for the tour, Karl Brazil, is not particularly associated with technology, being known as an acoustic drum kit performer primarily. On the tour he had to consider the breadth of Williams's work from boy band pop with Take That of the 1990s, through various genres up to the present-day releases. To be able to cope with the distinctive drum sounds associated with these records over a twenty-year span, Brazil's only option was to use technology. His live setup therefore incorporated the usual acoustic drum kit with Roland triggers on an acoustic snare and bass drum, as well as a Roland SPD-SX, which allows original drum samples from the recorded track to be loaded and triggered live. This allows an excellent hybrid of electronic and acoustic sounds.

In today's industry, such an approach is commonplace to varying degrees, and of course largely dependent on genre. A traditional jazz performance will probably need a four-piece kit with a couple of cymbals. But anything that leans toward pop, dance, or even metal will need an understanding of some of the equipment below.

Here I have split the equipment into four main parts:

1. electronic kits,
2. acoustic triggers,
3. sample pads, and
4. DAW software.

1. Electronic Kits

Gigs involving solely electronic kits are quite rare. Certainly if an acoustic sound is needed, then electronic drums won't deliver this authentically. Despite this, they are sometimes used due to space or noise limitations. They may therefore be necessary for some theater gigs or private functions, to give two examples. Where the music is very heavily electronic, an acoustic kit might not be called upon at all, with purely synthetic sounds needed, which are best supplied by the electronic kit. In either case, it is important to know how to navigate through the kit's computer system to find the correct sounds and do it quickly. It is also important to know how to play the kit. The response is different; the sensitivity (although very adaptable if you have time to set it up) is quite different from acoustic drums. It requires a slightly different approach. Modern kits from the big brands such as Roland and Yamaha offer so many options to modify sounds and sensitivity that you will need some time to come to grips with this before use in a professional environment.

2. Acoustic Triggers

These are much more common than full electronic kits in a live environment. As mentioned with Karl Brazil previously, these are positioned on acoustic drums so that when you hit the drum, it also sends an electronic signal via the trigger to your sound module so that you simultaneously produce the "real" drum sound as well as the chosen synthetic or sampled sound. When playing a smaller venue, the acoustic sounds would be very audible, so the triggered sound will be used to

Figure 5.8.

fatten up your acoustic sound or blend with it to give it a different character. If playing a very large venue, the acoustic sound can be omitted from the PA system and the audience will only hear the triggered sounds so you have more versatility. Many high-profile pop gigs will necessitate such a setup, and it is crucial to understand how this works and how you should play. You will need the discipline not to play ghost notes on the snare unless the sensitivity and velocity settings allow this, as a tiny ghost note might inadvertently trigger a full volume backbeat that will sound disastrous in the wrong place. As well as in pop, we see triggers of this kind increasingly used in other genres such as heavy metal. With so many lightning-fast bass drum notes being played, triggered sample sounds are often employed to allow the clarity of notes to cut through the music. You will also need to understand the equipment that produces the sounds as discussed in the next two points.

3. Sample Pads

Also discussed with Karl Brazil's setup, these are produced by many manufacturers such as Roland, Yamaha, Akai, Korg, and Alesis. The common design is a rectangular panel with several rubber pads that are struck by your regular

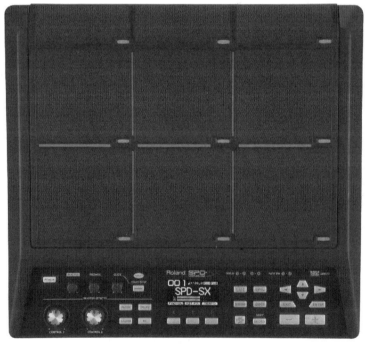

Figure 5.9.

drumstick. Each pad is assigned a different sound. One common use on stage is a particular snare sound, especially when a synthetic sound is required. Here the drummer might play his acoustic hi-hat and bass drum, while playing the sampled backbeat on the sample pad. Again, you need to understand how these feel to play and what you can play on them; the intricacies of your fastest rudiments won't sound very good. You also need to understand how to set these up. Will you use factory-supplied sounds? Will you import sounds? Will you use actual stems from the album version of the track? Each pad can be assigned a different sound and that configuration can be saved in the onboard memory. Several configurations might be able to be saved so you can switch sound sets for each song. Will you be able to switch between songs? Will you have a drum tech who controls that? Make sure you know the logistics thoroughly before performing to an audience.

4. DAW Software.

This acronym represents a digital audio workstation and includes well-known products such as Cubase, Pro Tools, and Logic Pro. This is the software that is run on a computer in most studios today, whether it's a high-end commercial studio or your bedroom setup. These are also regularly used on stage through laptops. These might provide backing tracks or samples, and nine times out of ten it is the drummer who will control such technology. Not only will you need a very good working knowledge of the equipment so that the show can run smoothly, but you will now have to keep on top of the flow of the live show so there are not uncomfortable pauses between songs while you find the right file and press the "play" button. When it comes to the studio use, a drummer that can produce is more useful than just a drummer. Learn the recording equipment inside out and you will develop the skills that help you become an asset as a producer and possible songwriter. You will also find yourself in the position to run your own drum sessions from your remote studio, a practice that is growing every year. Here you will be able to engineer and produce a drum track that you can send to a client through the Internet. Without knowledge of the technology, these avenues will not present themselves to you.

Of course another aspect of technology that is absolutely crucial for a drummer is the ability to play with a metronome. If there is any element of samples or backing tracks being performed live, then it will be the drummer who has the primary responsibility to keep in time with this. It may or may not be your job to start the sequences, change patches for each track, and so forth, but it will often be you who has it in your ears. This requirement is as important, if not more so, in the studio where much is played to the click, as discussed in an earlier chapter. Ignore the metronome at your peril!

CHAPTER 6

Health Strategies

SECRET 31: PROTECTING YOUR GREATEST INSTRUMENT

As musicians our ears are one of our greatest assets and yet many drummers abuse these vital pieces of "equipment" and take them for granted, despite common occurrences of such symptoms as tinnitus.

Deriving from the Latin meaning "to ring," tinnitus is a condition that affects our hearing and can become so severe that it can end a drummer's career.

What Is Tinnitus?

The human ear is a remarkable instrument consisting of the outer ear, middle ear, and inner ear. Between these three components, the ear can take the sound waves that it catches and turn them into electrical signals that the brain can compute as sound. Unfortunately this incredible organ can suffer damage from the very thing it is designed to detect.

Many of us have experienced temporary tinnitus after a concert, detected as a ringing in the ears that disappears by the following morning. If this noise exposure continues, then permanent damage can occur.

One symptom is the damage of the tiny hair cells in the inner ear, resulting in the loss of hearing of certain frequencies. This can occur in the frequencies of human speech, meaning that hearing parts of a conversation become difficult.

A second symptom of noise exposure is tinnitus. This is caused by the damaged hair cells transmitting a new signal to the brain. If this new signal is perceived by the brain as a sound, then a constant sound will be experienced inside the sufferer's head, often in the form of a high-pitched ringing or buzzing.

Around 20 percent of people suffer from tinnitus[1] and, as drummers, we stand a greater chance of being part of that statistic due to the fact that we strike things with wooden sticks to create loud noises. Add to this the environments of noisy concerts, deafening rehearsal rooms, and overly loud distorted guitar amps, and we have a real need to take action before permanent damage is caused.

What Is Too Loud?

To examine whether or not your environment is too noisy, there are two simple methods.

The first is to ascertain if the noise exposure you experience leaves you with ringing ears afterward. If it does, then you are experiencing tinnitus. This is known as temporary threshold shift and is a manifestation of your inner ear hair cells' fatigue from excessive noise.

The second method involves determining whether or not you can hold a conversation. As a rough guide see the list below:

- loud voice at 4 ft: 93 db
- shout at 4 ft: 99 db
- shout at 2 ft: 105 db
- impossible even close to listener's ear: over 110 db

What many people don't realize is that for every three-decibel increase, the safe exposure time is halved. This means that as 85 db is considered safe for a full working day (eight hours), the decibel increase and safe exposure time would look like this:

85 db: 8 hrs
88 db: 4 hrs
91 db: 2 hrs
94 db: 1 hr
97 db: 30 mins
100 db: 15 mins
103 db: 7.5 mins
106 db: 3.75 mins

Cure

There is currently not a cure for tinnitus so once the damage is done, it is here to stay.

Prevention

If you are employed as a musician, there are certain responsibilities that your employer has to ensure you are safe at work. These involve hearing protection, exposure time limits, suitable rest periods, available advice, and other forms of noise reduction. However, if you are a freelance or amateur drummer, then you don't have the luxury of someone considering your health. Therefore the responsibility lies with you.

Here are some tips for preventing hearing damage:

1. The best method of prevention would be to avoid noisy situations, but as a drummer that just isn't an option.
2. A more practical alternative is to limit your exposure time. During a rehearsal session, incorporate breaks in which you find somewhere quiet to rest your ears. During a performance, use the intermission to find a quiet space and rest those ears. When recording, between takes find somewhere quiet and rest your ears.
3. Stay hydrated to maintain inner ear function, and avoid alcohol as this affects the fluids in the inner ear.
4. Turn down. This will not always be possible, but you might want to consider whether the rehearsal really needs to be carried out at high volume. Often by turning down, you will find greater clarity in sound and the music might actually feel better, enabling band members to bounce off each other and create better music. A double whammy!
5. Wear hearing protection. The stigma of earplugs not being "cool" is finally fading as people start to realize that loss of hearing and tinnitus are even less cool. Most professional musicians use hearing protection now and a huge range of products exist on the market.

Range of Hearing Protection Products

When it comes to earplugs, most drummers hate them. They are often uncomfortable and cut out too much of certain frequencies and not enough of others, resulting in a muffled, unpleasant sound that sees us ripping them out halfway through the first song. But if you invest your money to buy a suitable pair, you will find a product that protects your ears and allows you to enjoy your music.

Products range from cheap disposable foam plugs for $1, moldable silicone plugs at around $3, plastic earplugs around $6, shooting muffs around $20, stereo isolation headphones around $60, custom-molded earplugs for around $100, and up to in ear monitors (IEM) for around $200.

Interestingly, we drummers will happily part with $200 for a Zildjian K dark crash cymbal but begrudge having to spend even $20 on hearing protection. But for all the enjoyment we can get out of our favourite drums and cymbals, they are nothing without a good pair of ears through which we can actually hear them.

Our ears are our greatest instrument, and spending money on keeping them maintained is one of the greatest investments you can make as a musician.

Obviously, it depends upon your application as to what you buy. Shooting ear muffs might have a great db reduction that work for practicing in your bedroom but might not fit the appropriate image on stage, so a discreet set of custom-molded earplugs might meet your needs.

If you play live and want the on-stage monitor sound to come direct into your ear at a safe volume, then IEMs would be a great choice. The custom fit means that they shut out much of the sound outside so you have complete control over the volume that reaches your ear through the monitors. Furthermore, the custom fit means they are comfortable, even when used for long periods.

Whatever you choose, by taking these steps to protect your ears, you will be able to go on enjoying music up to a ripe old age.

SECRET 32: LOOKING AFTER YOUR BACK

Drummers are at high risk of developing back pain, whether it's from hours on the stool with poor posture or lifting heavy equipment in and out of venues. Many of us accept this as an inevitable consequence of our art form, but a few simple steps can keep you playing pain free for many more years.

When lifting equipment, it is crucial to lift carefully with a straight back, bending from the knees and keeping the weight close to your body. When tired after a long gig, these good habits are easily replaced by lazy ones, bending over the bass drum and lifting it for example. Over time this takes its toll on your back.

The playing aspects, however, need to be looked at in slightly more depth. As it is only muscular strain, it can often be easily cured by changing the fundamentals of your playing. Doctor of chiropractic and director of the Chiropractic Performing Arts Network Timothy Jameson explains:

> The spine is a dynamic organ that responds to physical, chemical, and emotional stress throughout your lifetime. Physical stresses are problems like postural distortions, previous auto injuries, previous sports related injuries, falls, forward head posture and cumulative traumas, such as repetitive drumming for hour upon hour. Chemical stress is what you are putting (or not putting) in your body. Put lousy foods in your body and you have poor health, as your spine is directly related to your health. Finally, a very important aspect of spinal health is your current and past emotional health. Your current emotional health directly impacts the way you hold your body. If you're suffering from depression or poor self-esteem, you will carry your body with a forward head posture and drooped shoulders. If you have severe emotional stress in your past, it can be stored within the neuro-muscular network and create chronic spinal stress.[2]

So your diet and emotional state play a big role in keeping your spine in good working order, but another crucial aspect is your posture. This is largely affected by your drum kit setup and seat position, which warrant a separate discussion (Secret 33).

Prevention

So assuming your posture, diet, and emotional issues are taken care of, and you are lucky enough to have avoided back pain thus far, here are some tips and various options to keep you on the right path.

Warm up.

An athlete would never burst into a sprint without a thorough warm-up and neither should a musician. Most players have their own preferred warm-up to avoid injury and ensure optimum performance. It may simply entail a sequence of rudiments, gradually increasing with speed. This is discussed in Secret 47.

Analyze your lifestyle.

Your drumming technique may be perfect, but that's no good if you're causing the damage elsewhere. Ensure good habits through every activity, for example, sport, computer usage, lifting, and so on.

Analyze your kit setup.

Make sure your kit is set up for maximum efficiency to avoid overstretching.

Stretch.

Every human should stretch their muscles, especially if you're involved in physical activity. Well-stretched gluteal muscles and hamstrings are important to maintain looseness, and lower back mobility exercises are crucial to avoid seizing up later in life. Below are four examples of lower mobility exercises.

1. Flexion Stretch: Lying on back with head on floor, pull one knee back to chest and hold for several seconds. Repeat with other knee.

Figure 6.1.

2. Flexion Stretch 2: Starting on all fours, bring buttocks down to heels. Hold for several seconds and repeat.

Figure 6.2.

3. Back Extension: Lie on back, knees bent up with head on a small pillow and arms out to the side in a crucifix position. Hold it for two minutes without allowing the lower back to arch.

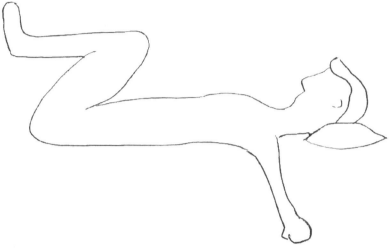

Figure 6.3.

4. Back Stabilization: Starting on all fours, stretch out right arm and left leg simultaneously, keeping back and neck straight. Hold for several seconds and repeat with opposite limbs.

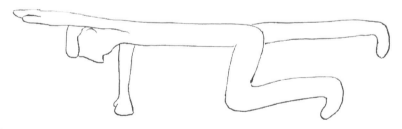

Figure 6.4.

Develop core muscle stability.

Our core muscles are often the key to great posture. With bad habits, these muscles wither, and so our back takes the strain, which in turn allows the muscles to wither even more. A vicious circle occurs. By developing these abdominal muscles, the back is relieved from this extra strain. Core muscles are not your six-pack, but the deeper muscles that sit behind them forming a band around the tummy. You strengthen these by tensing in the same way you would upon entering a cold sea. You should aim to hold that tension for 10 seconds while allowing maintained, natural breathing. There are many other exercises to develop the entire core muscle strength, and these can be found with an Internet search or visit to a GP.

Meditate.

Increasingly, physiotherapists are suggesting meditation as a method of correcting physical problems such as back pain. A mass of books and CDs, such as *Meditation for Optimum Health: How to Use Mindfulness and Breathing to Heal Your Body and Refresh Your Mind*, are available to talk about the benefits of this and how to put it into action.

Study the Alexander Technique.

This technique is very popular with many musicians. Lessons are undertaken and your specific needs are addressed through a method that releases harmful tension by coordinating the mind and body. This also vastly improves posture and general health.

Study the Feldenkrais Method.

This method as taught at Berklee College of Music is a system that allows the body to move and function more efficiently and comfortably. It can re-educate the nervous system and improve motor ability while relieving pressure on joints, allowing the body to heal repetitive strain injuries. Continued use of the method can relieve pain and lead to higher standards of achievement in music.

Cure

If you're one of the many who suffers from back pain already, here are some options that might help you get back to pain-free drumming.

Acupuncture

A Chinese method with a 2,000-year history, acupuncture involves thin needles pushed into specific points in the body thought to correspond to certain organs and anatomic areas deep inside.

Chiropractor

The chiropractic philosophy is that realigning the spine relieves pressure on the spinal nerves, which can help restore natural nerve function throughout the body. They believe a well-aligned body is more naturally balanced and therefore less pain is experienced.

Osteopaths

Osteopaths believe the body is an integrated, biological system. As a result, problems in one area of the body can adversely affect other areas. The function and structure are closely related, so by correcting the structure, the body will function properly.

Massage therapy

Studies have shown massage to improve range of motion, blood circulation, and levels of endorphins.

Yoga

Yoga develops muscular endurance and flexibility through stretches that allow the muscles to be strengthened.

Spinal surgery

Surgery is usually considered a last option as 95 percent of patients with low back pain can benefit from nonoperative methods.

How to choose

Back pain is still not fully understood and different professionals from different practices will offer contradicting opinions and cures.

As a result, there is no single cure for every sufferer and each individual really needs to try different methods to see what works. Find out which treatments are covered by health insurance and start with those to avoid the expense.

Whatever your situation, it is important to play with correct posture so you can enjoy a long and painless life of drumming.

Relevant Books

The Athletic Musician: A Guide to Playing Without Pain by Harrison Christine

Playing (Less) Hurt: An Injury Prevention Guide for Musicians by Janet Horvath

Body Learning: An Introduction to the Alexander Technique by Michael J. Gelb

The Alexander Technique (2000) by Jane Kosminsky and Deborah Caplan

Musician's Injuries: A Guide to their Understanding and Prevention by Nicola Culf

The Musician's Survival Manual by R. Norris

SECRET 33: OPTIMIZING SETUP AND SEAT POSITION

It is all too easy to overlook the aspect of efficient drum kit configuration and stool height, what with setting up and packing down our drum kit night after night, practicing for hours and hours, and simply not stopping to consider if we are damaging our bodies and making hard work for ourselves.

Incorrect stool height can place severe strain on our spine, the wrong distance to the pedals can cause us significantly more work to play certain patterns, and overstretching for drums can cause injury and poor performance.

Therefore, taking an hour to really consider this and adjust the ergonomics of our kit can actually save hours of inefficient playing and potential injury.

To look at each aspect carefully, I have divided them up into factors that concern our health and well-being and factors that inhibit our playing potential or that need attention depending on what we play, though many will of course overlap.

Health

Stool height/Distance to pedals

As drummers come in many different shapes and sizes, each player's setup should be individual, enabling them to play the instrument with ease while avoiding unnecessary stretching. The optimal height for a drum throne is when it allows you to sit with your knees level or slightly below your hips and both feet sit on the pedals several inches in front of your knees. If you are too close to the pedals, it will restrict control of your foot movements. If your knees are too high, it encourages poor posture and causes back pain.

Jameson comments: "The position of the seat in relation to the drum kit is very important. A movement of an inch or two in either direction can be essential in keeping spinal and muscular balance."[3]

Height of drums/Amount of stretch to drums/Posture

Why do some people manage to play for several decades without any problems when others can't avoid the agony in a single practice session? Nicholas Quarrier, clinical associate professor at Ithaca College, says, "The answer to this million dollar question may be that repetitious activity is not injurious by itself unless it is performed in an abnormal stressful posture. More importantly, the abnormal stressed posture may be the cause of a large percentage of music-related injuries."[4]

To sit correctly while drumming is no different from any other activity. You should be upright with a straight back with your shoulders above your hips. To find the correct posture, sit on the stool and completely slouch. Now straighten

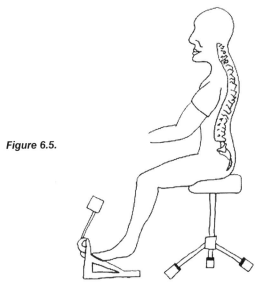

Figure 6.5.

your back as much as possible with an overexaggerated lower back curve. You can then release the position very slightly to find the perfect position. This may feel very strange if you are used to slouching, but by doing this process, it may highlight the extreme difference between correct posture and slouching. This way your core muscles are supporting your body rather than your spine doing the work. Instead of scrunching forward, your arms and shoulders should hang naturally and relaxed with your weight distributed evenly across both hips.

Once you have the seat and pedals set correctly, and have established a good posture, you can start to position the snare, toms, and cymbals. Because of our difference in body shapes and dimensions, each individual will have a unique optimum setup, but the basic rule is that you shouldn't need to stretch for anything. This will bring on fatigue and increase the risk of strains and injuries. Examine where your stick/arm movement naturally wants to strike the snare drum and position it there. Work out the tom and cymbal positions in the same way. Position the kit to fit your body rather than struggling to fit your body to the kit.

Another trick that helps some drummers to achieve an upright spine involves raising the back of the seat by about 15 or 20 degrees. This is easily achieved with a block of wood under the back legs. This position encourages correct lumbar curve, and sitting up so tall prevents the flattening of your diaphragm and collapsing of your chest, which limits full breathing.

As well as posture, the way you incorporate muscular movement in your playing can also prevent injury. A useful exercise from Dr. Jameson is to "check the muscular tension in your neck while playing slower beats. Now play at 150bpm and check how much tension you are carrying throughout your body as the speed increases."

This improved posture also encourages deeper breathing, which helps keep us calm and oxygenates our muscles.

Playing Factors

Distance between drums/Angle of toms, snare, cymbals/Height of hi-hat

When looking at the drum kits of drummers from different genres, we will notice some big differences. It is important to consider the reasons behind these differences when setting your own kit up for different situations. I will use a different setup for jazz to that of a rock gig, simply because the sound I want to achieve is done so more easily with certain setup changes.

The distance between your drums is often determined by how much movement you will be making to generate power and the type of fills or beats you will be performing.

A heavy rock drummer might be making overexaggerated arm movements while playing heavy, powerful, and yet quite spacious fills. This drummer might feel that he wants more space to maneuver, and therefore the toms may be more spaced out. His left hand might move high up for each backbeat, and therefore his hi-hat might be positioned vertically further from his snare drum to avoid his hands colliding. He may be coming down from a greater height on to his toms, and therefore they may be positioned at quite a flat angle.

On the other hand, a jazz drummer might find himself playing many more fast, intricate notes with much less power. His priority is moving quickly and smoothly around the drums, and therefore a more compact setup might be preferable.

Another consideration might be less orthodox approaches. Simon Phillips used to play with a very low hi-hat that sat level with his snare head on some occasions, and this worked incredibly well for his open-handed approach.

Drum Configuration

Looking further into unorthodox configurations of the drums and cymbals, you could examine a great pioneer in this field: Bill Bruford. At one time his drum kit consisted of two flat lines; line one had a snare in the middle and two toms on either side. The second line behind that had a hi-hat in the middle with symmetrical cymbal choices on either side. This symmetrical approach meant that both his hands had access to the same voices and therefore his approach could be different from every other drummer. Billy Cobham was a left-handed drummer who played open handed, so his toms were also unique and didn't follow the conventional pattern ranging from high to low.

SECRET 34: POTENTIAL HEALTH RISKS

We've discussed back pain and tinnitus as risks for drummers, but there are also several other health problems experienced commonly by drummers. These generally fall into one of two categories.

Traumatic Event Injuries

These one-off events can include striking yourself with a stick, falling, lifting equipment in the wrong way, breaking a stick, or a strain.

Overuse Injuries

Excessive burden on the tissues as a result of continual impact, gravitational force, and/or muscular contraction can cause inflammation. This swelling can alter the motion of the affected area and cause pain.

Below are some of the common problems experienced by drummers. As with any injury, prevention is much better than cure, but some steps to help heal are also included in case it is too late to prevent. This is just a guide and not a substitute for professional health advice. If any problems persist, seek professional advice immediately. Some conditions such as back pain can actually be a precursor to much more serious conditions.

Neck Pain

As a follow-up from the back pain discussions, the neck is also at risk of injury through bad posture and ineffective kit setup. If you are slouching, there is a strong chance that your head is also drooped forward, seemingly exiting your body from the front and not the top. This places severe strain on your neck muscles. Equally, if your drums are too far away, then you are constantly and potentially violently stretching for them and this can also lead to neck strain. Ensure that your straight back also allows an upright head position above your shoulders and that when you move around all parts of the kit, you can maintain this position.

If it already hurts, stop playing, rest for a few days but no longer, and alter your kit as prescribed in Secret 33. Ice the area immediately to reduce the chance of inflammation.

Blisters/Hand Pain

Blisters are a common complaint in drummers, but these are really only a natural reaction to sudden increases in friction. Try to build up slowly to a high playing level rather than going from very little playing to suddenly performing two-hour concerts. The blister will soon harden over, and a callus will form to protect that area of the hand. This is not a problem unless the callus is cracking, in which case it may need moisturizing.

Many hand injuries occur as a result of poor stick choice or poor technique. A very small drummer may suffer if he or she selected a large, heavy drumstick. This creates too much strain on the wrist and hand and therefore an unnatural technique might occur. Some drummers also play through the drumhead rather than using the rebound. The correct technique was discussed in Secret 12, but suffice to say that if you are striking the drum and then trying to push down beyond that impact point, great strain is placed upon your hand, wrist, and arm. This overly hard playing is not necessary, and the perceived need of this to create volume is misleading. With correct technique (not to mention microphone placement), a drummer can fill any concert hall or arena with enough noise.

Once again, try to rest the injury for a few days, examine your technique, and always try to build up slowly to a large performance time. The length and intensity of playing must be developed a little every day. If enduring long rehearsals, make sure you take regular breaks, keep hydrated, and do some stretches.

Neuritis

Drummers can experience brachial neuritis, which is irritation or infection along a nerve in the arm or wrist causing pain, weakness, or numbness. A sharp and sudden onset of pain can often first be felt in the upper arm or shoulder, although the wrist and fingers are not immune. It can also distort any of your senses. A physician should be consulted if any symptoms occur, but the usual correct, symmetrical setup and warm-up before playing can help prevent this.

Elbow Epicondylitis

The bony region inside the elbow is prone to great stress from the nearby tendons and fascia, which are very active when drumming. Inflammation can occur, resulting in severe elbow pain.

Certain stretches, ultrasound therapy, massage, and joint mobilization techniques are sometimes used after the event.

Sufficient warm-ups and stretching are key to preventing this injury. Proper technique is again essential as excessive elbow force when drumming can be a cause. Allowing the stick to rebound lessens this force.

Carpal Tunnel Syndrome

The median nerve passes through the carpal tunnel on the palm side of our wrist and serves our thumb and second finger by controlling motion and allowing sensation. If this nerve is compressed as a result of hypertension or inflammation, then we experience carpal tunnel syndrome in the form of pain or loss of sensation.

Commonly experienced by drummers, it is caused by vibration and tight gripping. This is difficult to avoid when drumming, and over time, the repetitive nature of this takes its toll. It is not necessarily the result of poor technique, but more the repeated vibrating nature of playing the drums, although there are also hereditary genetic factors in many cases.

To help decrease the chances of this, stretch the neck, shoulders, forearms, wrist, and fingers before playing. Stretches can also assist in recovery from the syndrome, although surgery is often necessary.

Drumming can be a cause of carpal tunnel syndrome, but it can also indicate other problems such as diabetes or obesity so a health professional consultation would be wise.

Tendonosis/Tendonitis

This problem for drummers involves a tendon and its sheath becoming irritated and swelling up to begin healing. This can lead to a build-up of fluids, as well as pain and loss of motion. This can occur through overuse of the arm and shoulder, especially if continually riding on a cymbal that requires stretching to reach.

The best way to minimize the chance of this is to set the kit up to lessen excessive stretching, always warm up before playing, and ensure good technique when playing.

Once a problem has occurred, stop playing, ice the area, and rest for a couple of days. Then gentle stretching and mobilization exercises might help condition the affected limb and enable you to play the drums again with correct technique and warm-ups. More severe cases might require a specialist physiotherapist.

Strain

Strains exist when muscle or soft tissue fibers sustain a tear. These can range from a few damaged fibers up to whole muscles. These are usually a result of excessive load placed upon a muscle, tendon, or fascia when the tissue was in a rest period and not ready for intense action.

In other words, launching into a frenzied drum solo from cold is not advised. Once again, good stretching, diet, and conditioning of the body will allow you the greatest chance of avoiding such an injury.

If the strain has occurred already, stop playing, ice the area, and rest it. Keep treating with ice for a couple of days and then begin gentle exercise to increase the range of motion and allow the scar tissue to form correctly.

NOTES

1. "About tinnitus," American Tinnitus Association, http://www.ata.org/for-patients/about-tinnitus (accessed May 27, 2013).

2. Timothy Jameson, e-mail message to author, January 2, 2008.

3. Timothy Jameson, e-mail message to author, January 2, 2008.

4. Nicholas Quarrier, e-mail message to author, February 4, 2010.

CHAPTER 7

Preparation Strategies

SECRET 35: WRITING CHARTS QUICKLY

As working musicians, we often have to learn a large amount of material in a very short space of time and then perform it as if we've been playing it for years. Ideally we would immerse ourselves in the music for a longer period of time until we know every note, every fill, and every time signature change inside out. But often this is just not possible with short deadlines and other work commitments. And so the easiest answer is to grab the manuscript pad and write things down.

However, the act of transcribing a drum part can itself be very time consuming and therefore actually take away time that you could have been practicing the parts at the kit. So here are some tips to help you write drum charts quickly.

Firstly, minimize the information that you need. Sometimes I know a track well enough once it's started, but I may not feel confident that I will remember the tempo and the initial groove when we reach that song in the set. In this case I might simply write the song title, tempo, and first bar of groove. That will get me started and then the rest of the song will just flow out from my memory.

If that information isn't quite adequate, I will see what else is needed. There might be a specific ending, so write that down. There might be a few tricky bars in the middle eight, so write that down. But if the rest of the song is easy to remember, leave the page blank for those parts so you can focus on playing the song and not staring at all the dots on the page.

Sometimes, however, you just won't know the song at all and will need cues throughout. Below are two examples of charts that I have written in the past.

The first one is "Come Fly with Me" by Frank Sinatra. Straight away you will see the title and the symbol that tells us that this song is swung. We are then given a groove for three bars and then a stop. After this you will find that the groove is only given again when it changes or at the beginning of a new section. Otherwise we just have repeats and rhythm slashes to tell us how many bars to keep grooving. This avoids unnecessary ink on the page, and thus less information to process.

Another aspect of this song is the ensemble stabs that we see written above some of the bars, such as bar 18. This tells us that the whole band is hitting those notes so we might also want to emphasize this. It doesn't tell us what to play it on so as drummers we have a musical choice to make here. As you gain more experience, you will feel it in the music whether you should play a huge accent or a subtle touch on these notes. You can also look for dynamic markings in these situations or whether the note is long (maybe play a cymbal) or short (maybe play a staccato snare).

And so other than these repeats and ensemble stabs, the only other information are actual stops in the music such as bar 25 or the end of the piece. This type of chart is very easy to read. It is not cluttered but does give us all the necessary information so we could sit down and play this song correctly without a rehearsal.

The second example is a very basic, handwritten chart from a recording session I did at my drum studio. Having heard the song a couple of times, I want to get on the drums to find the right sounds and experiment with fills and grooves. I don't want to spend hours learning the track.

So here I scribble out the simplest chart I can. This one starts with a two-bar rest for me, then I play six bars of sixteenth note hi-hats and a quarter note (four-on-the-floor) bass drum pattern. This information is conveyed with two bars on the page. I also jot down that on the final bar of that intro I should do a fill. No need to write a fill out as I don't know what I will play yet and I'd rather just feel it.

We then have the main groove of the song. I only write this out once in the whole track as the same type of groove is used for every section, as requested by the client. I will most likely adapt it to differentiate between the sections and create lifts in the music, but I won't detail this in the drum chart. Remember that I want to write drum charts quickly, so it is important to minimize the information written.

The next stage is to reveal the structure of the track. The main groove here plays for eight bars, as shown with "X8." We then have "V1" to denote verse one. I know it's the same groove so I simply write "X16." I now know that I should play that groove for sixteen bars, but within that I might add extra bass drums, a fill, or whatever else I think the music needs. This doesn't need to be written though.

We then hit the chorus, which is just eight more bars of that groove. I will possibly play this at a higher intensity, but again, I don't need to write that down for myself. After the chorus there are four bars with accents on beat 1 and 4&. These are therefore written out and between them I want to do a fill so I simply write "FILL" and then I'll improvise something.

We then have another identical verse and chorus so just the number of bars is written again. The next section is a guitar solo or "Git Solo." Here I will play the

Figure 7.1. **Studio session chart**

same beat but on the ride with the bell being accented on the off-beats. To keep it simple you will notice on the chart that I have just written, "Ride off beat bell X8." I know exactly what that means and it won't take me long to process that when I read it.

We then have a double chorus which simply says "X16" and then another groove like the intro for four bars, the last one having a stab to end the track. So here we can just write the groove with "X3" and then in the last bar simply write in the final stab, just including rhythm slashes for the remainder of the bar, which is the same as the previous three bars.

This shorthand-type approach is crucial to getting the job done quickly. Only including necessary information also allows you to play the drums more freely rather than being mentally tied to an intricate drum chart.

The only way to get good at this process is to do it, and certainly the way I learned to write drum charts was by sitting down with a pen and manuscript pad and working through the music. So as an exercise, try picking a track that you don't really know and see how well you can capture all the necessary information on some paper. Then try playing through the track and see if you can understand what you have written. This type of exercise will really help you next time you need to learn a set for a gig that's happening tomorrow, or when you're in the studio with a song to play that you've never heard before.

Figure 7.2.

SECRET 36: NAILING THE AUDITION

I haven't met many musicians who enjoy the audition process. They can be incredibly nerve-racking environments and cause us to feel inhibited, tense, sweaty, scared, unrehearsed, unsure of what is expected, and distracted by minor things that normally go unnoticed. Not ideal reactions to a situation in which we're supposed to demonstrate how good we are at playing our instrument.

If you suffer from these problems, they can be overcome, and maybe the best remedy is just to get out there and gain experience by attending auditions and becoming comfortable with the process.

But there are certain steps that we should take to ensure we have the best chance of being successful at every audition.

1. Do your research.

The more you know about the gig, the better you can prepare. What music is it? What equipment will you need? Which cymbals, drums, sticks? What style of playing should you brush up on? What should you wear? What sort of people will you be trying to impress? It all helps to understand what is required.

2. Prepare, prepare, and then prepare some more.

I've never gone into a musical situation and thought, "Damn, I overprepared. I know all the music, I feel relaxed, and I'm playing really well. What a fool!" But I have definitely gone into many situations wishing I had had more chance to practice or more knowledge of what was required. Learn the music if you can. Get recordings, make your own charts, and practice until you know it in your sleep. Also on the logistics side of things, where is the rehearsal studio for the audition? Where can you park? What gear will they provide? Make sure you leave nothing to chance that will ruffle your feathers.

3. Arrive early.

Promptness is one of the biggest aspects that we hear top musicians talk about all the time. Don't be the one who keeps everyone waiting, especially if you have a drum kit to set up. Get there early, get relaxed, and be ready when they call you.

4. Warm up.

Warm up. You only have one chance to make a first impression, so don't let it be one of a wooden, stiff-sounding nervous wreck. Even if you just take a practice pad and go through your regular warm-up routine, just do it. Limber up and focus your mind, and the act of playing will help relax you too.

5. Act confidently.

Even if you're shaking inside, project a confident and competent persona and you will come across in a much better light. That doesn't mean you have to overdo it and steal the show, but remember that you're auditioning to be a performer who can get up on a stage and perform.

6. Be yourself—personable.

Be a nice person. Why would anyone want to choose a difficult person to spend all their time with? A huge part of the job doesn't involve drumming but more your impact on the creative environment. Are you a positive person who will lift the session or a negative person that will bring people down and cause distraction?

It's like the saying, "Some people light up a room when they enter it; some people light up a room when they leave it." Which would you want in your creative environment?

7. Stay relaxed.

The psychological enemy is often our worst enemy. Our brain is sometimes out to sabotage us and we have to learn how to control it. Practice relaxation techniques in the calm and peace of your own home so when you need to call on them, they are well rehearsed and have more chance of working. Maybe you have certain breathing exercises that help, maybe a certain drumming warm-up routine, maybe a visualization exercise. In the 2010 Dream Theater drummer auditions, successful applicant Mike Mangini spoke of how he considered every potential problem that could occur at the audition so that if it happened, he would be prepared. Whatever works for you, just make sure when you're there you can focus on the music and have fun doing what you love doing.

8. Take "essential" equipment.

It is often impractical to take a whole drum kit to an audition, which poses an obstacle that guitarists and singers may not share; the instrument that we play will be unfamiliar and quite possibly substandard. However, it is always worth taking some key elements of the drum kit to reduce this potentially damaging situation and allow us to focus on doing our job well. Such elements may include cymbals, snare drum, and a bass drum pedal.

From my own experience, many years ago I traveled to a downtrodden rehearsal studio in West London for an audition. I took very little with me, and when I sat at the kit, I found that the bass pedal was not only bad; it was nearly unplayable. There was no time to take it apart and try to get it working, so I just had to play. In a pressurized situation, a nervous audition in which I had to sight-read music that I didn't know, this just distracted me further, left me flustered, and caused me to play terribly. I began reading notes wrong and making bad decisions, such as going to the ride cymbal at a completely inappropriate time.

As the MD and agent smiled and said goodbye, I knew I had let it slip away. I left the room and smiled wearily at the next drummer waiting for his audition. I looked down and saw his stick bag, his cymbals, his snare drum, and his well-maintained and perfectly playable bass drum pedal. Lesson learned the hard way for me.

9. Try to work out what they want.

Maybe the hardest thing to ascertain is what they really want. Do they want someone to interpret the music in his or her own way? Do they want someone to play it note for note like the record (if you are joining an existing band or show)? Do they just want someone who looks good even if they can't offer much musically? In reference to the aforementioned Dream Theater audition, some of those world-class drummers played the old parts as the previous drummer, Mike Portnoy, had. Others chose to interpret the parts slightly differently, and it transpired that the band really wanted the original parts maintained as that was what they were used to and what the fans wanted to hear. See if you can work out if technical ability, sight-reading, stage presence and showmanship, or timekeeping and groove are the key to your audition.

10. Don't be disheartened.

Although it may sound negative, it is a reality that not everybody can be successful in every audition. I doubt there are any successful musicians who don't have a failed audition story to tell. But if it happens to you, get over it. It doesn't mean you're a bad drummer. It doesn't mean you're a terrible person. It might be that you had the wrong-colored hair, wore the wrong T-shirt, didn't twirl your sticks enough, twirled your sticks too much! Who knows what they wanted? The best thing you can do is take note of anything that you could improve on (such as my bass pedal experience) and make sure you don't do it again. Otherwise forget about it, get back to the practice room, and look forward to the next opportunity. Keep improving, keep going for auditions, and your chance will come.

SECRET 37: FINANCIAL PLANNING

Some drummers are fortunate enough to make vast sums of money from their musical endeavors. Others might make a more modest income but will have the security of a year-round gig that pays consistently. But for many the work will be sporadic, and this can make planning and progressing in life difficult when finances are concerned.

Unfortunately, many musicians are also not particularly knowledgeable or interested in proper financial planning and can frequently find themselves in difficult situations when bill payments are being demanded.

However, just because you don't have a set salary or regular paychecks, life doesn't need to be a hand-to-mouth affair. With a little organization and sensible spending, you can enjoy a much more secure financial situation.

This brief article is not a substitute for a professional financial advisor, but will hopefully highlight a few areas that you should be considering.

Emergency Fund

It is tempting to spend your hard-earned money as soon as it appears in your bank account, but it is very sensible to build an emergency bank fund for the unforeseen events that do and will occur. You may need a new washing machine, some parts for your car, a boiler repair, or a number of other things that will happen at some point in your life. But it also may be required for a time when you are ill or injured and cannot work. A self-employed musician doesn't enjoy benefits such as sick pay so you must be ready for this. These are incredibly stressful events for the unprepared, but the sensible forward thinkers with an emergency fund can afford the bill without worry.

Aim to have three to six months' expenses in the bank. If your work is seasonal, you may require more. You might wish to store this money in a USA Money Market Account or a UK tax free ISA account where you can earn some interest but also have easy access. Each country will offer different options so do some research or speak to a financial advisor.

Retirement Fund

Retirement can seem like a faraway event that can be dealt with later in life. But as a self-employed person, you should start contributing to a retirement plan as soon as possible. The more you pay in, the greater the payouts upon retirement. If you leave it until you are in your forties, you only have twenty years of payments to provide your income for the rest of your life. If you start in your twenties, then you have double the time to spread out the payments. Even if you can only afford a small amount, it is worth starting the plan and then increasing the payments as you can afford them.

Income Protection

Income protection (or income replacement) schemes might seem like another drain on your limited funds, but they are well worth considering. If you have dependents, then it could be argued that it is foolhardy not to have something like this in place. These plans are there to give you monthly payouts if you become unable to work through injury or illness.

You need to set the payouts to cover all of your necessary expenses such as the mortgage, utility bills, and so on. You can also set the time at which this policy comes into effect after the injury. The longer the time lapse, the smaller the premiums. If you have an emergency fund to cover you for six months, then you can set your payment protection plan to start after six months and the premium will be much lower than if it started after only a month.

Speak to your financial advisor to understand all the current products available to you.

Life Insurance

This is a big one for the family person. If you have a spouse and children that rely on your income, then you need to make sure that there is some cover for them if you die. It's unpleasant to think about this, but death is a reality, and your most precious people will be left in a sorry situation if this is not put in place.

Taxes

As a working musician, it is imperative to consider your work as a business and not just a hobby. It is very easy to think that those cash-in-hand gigs are not traceable or significant and therefore you shouldn't declare it.

The problem is that if you are making a reasonable living from your music, then it starts to look slightly suspect if you are not producing convincing accounts each year, and musicians and music teachers are being targeted more and more by the tax enforcers.

At the very least, keep a spreadsheet of all your income. Keep invoices, records of dates and venues, and anything else that makes your income easy to follow.

At the end of the tax year, make sure you've got a good accountant who can help you produce what you need. A good accountant might cost a little money, but he or she will also help you save money by finding tax breaks that you might not even know about.

Expenses

As a self-employed musician, you are able to deduct business expenses for many items that you have purchased for your business. Any musical equipment, stage clothes, travel costs, union or other association subscriptions, food at work, and anything else that is work related will be tax deductible.

Keep all receipts and add the items into another column on your spreadsheet. Some people have a hellish week at the end of the tax year when they have to sift through a year's worth of receipts and invoices. Another option is to spend ten minutes every week processing the past week's materials and keep on top of it. This can then all go to the accountant for him or her to work with.

Your tax person might even find asset depreciation (such as your car or drum kits) among other areas to save you tax.

CHAPTER 8

Marketability Strategies

SECRET 38: LEARN ALL STYLES TO PASSABLE LEVEL

This may not sound particularly professional on the face of it as surely we would want to be a master of every conceivable style. But for most mortals we will find our strengths in a few areas.

I know some amazing jazz drummers who just don't sound great when they play rock, even though the rock drumming might often seem less complex than their preferred jazz rhythms. They can play the correct notes in the correct order, but they lack the power, energy, and decision making in that genre that a rock drummer would find instinctive. Of course, I also know many great rock drummers who fall apart when asked to play jazz.

This is not necessarily a problem if you can carve a decent career within a single genre, but I am a firm believer that a musician who wants a sustainable career in the music industry must be able to perform convincingly at every opportunity. After all, you might take a jazz gig and find yourself backstage with a rock 'n' roll legend who offers you a gig in his band based upon your recent jazz performance. As long as you're out there performing and promoting the brand of "you," then opportunities will present themselves.

But beyond that, even when playing a certain genre, the music often stretches into other genres. One example is a recent gig that I depped on. The band was primarily reggae, a style which I love and feel comfortable playing. We had one rehearsal before the show and I had two days to learn the set before that rehearsal. Within that set I found myself playing reggae, jazz, drum and bass, funk, dubstep, go-go, samba, and heavy rock.

That was no problem; I am au fait with all of those drumming styles. But had I struggled with any of them, I would not have had time to learn them to the required performance standard, the show would have suffered, and I wouldn't have worked with any of those musicians again.

Another example that has happened on numerous occasions is the typical mid-performance jamming when playing in one style—let's say rock—and the MD shouts something along the lines of, "Go reggae!" Here you have all of two seconds to work out what you will play, how it will work at this tempo, and the all-important drum fill that will make the transition between styles sound effective. There is certainly no time to consult your "how to play reggae drums" manual.

My personal list of experiences when I have felt glad to have studied many styles could fill a book by itself, but one last example is gaining a seat in a musical or cruise ship orchestra. These types of jobs are notorious for throwing just about every style, tempo, and time signature at you; often all within the same song! It is a vital requirement to know your styles.

One of the big cruise ship companies devotes a section of their audition to hearing you play the following styles: swing, rumba, cha-cha, samba, Broadway show-2, swing ballad, and funk rock. This is simply to check that you can play a range of styles on the spot.

Below is a list of other styles that you should be sure to know. Hopefully you now understand why I do not think everyone should panic themselves into trying to master every style; this is not always possible. But making sure that you can play a few basic grooves of each style, play them at a range of tempos, and play in sequence with fills will ensure that you can make the right impression in every situation. Just make sure they sound authentic and convincing enough and you will get the job done. From there you can build on these skills, and if ever a show requires a deeper knowledge of a certain style, you will already have the foundations on which to build up to that level. Of course one of the best ways to really understand a style is to listen to the masters of that genre. Soak it up, absorb everything you hear and see, and then try to get in situations where you can play this music yourself, even if it's just jamming with friends.

Styles (Not a comprehensive list but a good starting point)

rock
funk
pop
disco
electronic/dance
drum and bass
hip-hop
jazz
jazz with brushes
punk

soul/Motown
reggae
bossa nova
samba
songo
mambo
show 2
salsa
cha-cha
Mozambique
heavy metal
blues—shuffle
Afro-beat
country

SECRET 39: FOCUS YOUR EFFORTS

We discussed time management for practice sessions in Secret 1, but we also need to manage our time well in all areas of our life. One of these areas is marketing ourselves. If we had a full-time marketing agency behind us, they could look at every possible avenue of marketing, analyze the cost and time effectiveness of each method, and constantly work toward getting you more work. But we don't have such luxuries so everything you do in this area takes time that could be spent practicing the drums, going to gigs, or even spending time with your loved ones. Remember them?

To help us focus on the task at hand, it is important to ascertain what you really want from your career. What is your ultimate goal?

Do you want to tour the world as a pop session drummer? Hold a seat in a big Broadway show? Teach on the drumming course at a well-respected music school? Write for your favourite musical publication? Become part of a band that writes a Grammy-winning album?

Once you have established your dream goal, you can then work out the most effective and efficient course of action to maximize your chances of reaching that goal. Not only will this enable you to focus your efforts, it will also feel incredibly motivating and empowering from the onset.

Here are some exercises to help discover what you truly want and then how to achieve it.

Exercise 1

Write a list of 10 important goals that you *still wish to achieve*. Make sure the number one goal is the ultimate dream goal, but then fill the list with nine other goals that you would love along the way. By stretching the list to ten, you will really have to think and get to know yourself more profoundly.

Exercise 2

List ten important goals that you have *already achieved* in your life. This helps to clearly discover what has been important to you so far, builds your confidence by remembering past successes, and helps to plan future goals.

Exercise 3

Write a list of ten ways that you achieved the *first goal* in Exercise 2.

Exercise 4

Write a list of ten ways that you achieved the *second goal* in Exercise 2.

Exercise 5

Write a list of ten ways that you achieved the *third goal* in Exercise 2, and so on. This helps us to work out the key actions that made those achievements happen. We are really focusing on the key events that helped you to success. Once you have finished Exercises 3–5, it is time to transfer this knowledge to help the future goals.

Exercise 6

Write a list of ten ways that you think you could achieve the *first goal* in Exercise 1.

Exercise 7

Write a list of ten ways that you think you could achieve the *second goal* in Exercise 1.

Exercise 8

Write a list of ten ways that you think you could achieve the *third goal* in Exercise 1.

Take your time writing these lists. It might flood out in one session, or you may take several days to really ponder. Once finished, put the lists aside for a few days and let the thoughts percolate in your mind as you process what you have learned about yourself and how you can take action to make things happen for you.

Armed with this life plan, it is now time to go out there and achieve your dreams.

SECRET 40: PROMOTING YOURSELF

"It's not what you know; it's who you know" goes the old adage, still very pertinent to musicians today. Of course, we do really need to know a fair bit as well to actually carry out the job once we get a chance, but we need to get our foot in the door first and foremost.

Networking is still a crucial aspect of being a full-time musician, and the wider the net of music industry people we know, the more chance we have of being offered work. And still the best way of networking is to get out there and play the drums with other musicians. Meeting with musicians, building relationships, allowing them to hear and see you play is the best advertisement for the brand of "you" in existence.

But if you live in an area with a poor music scene, then playing in the "Nag's Head" pub night after night might not feel like the best way to boost your career.

As musicians we would be foolish to ignore the numerous, increasing, and free networking platforms available to us via the Internet. This is a chance for us to interact with the world, share our music, connect with the right people, and get real-life opportunities that would otherwise be difficult to find.

Website

The first step is to have your own website. A few years ago this might not have been seen as essential, but today there is no excuse. It is the first place a person will go to check you out, and it's your chance to have a virtual shop window where you can show off your best recordings, videos, experience, photos, and anything else that promotes you. Furthermore it costs next to nothing. If budget is a major concern, then take the time to research website-building services such as Wordpress that allow total novices to produce professional-looking sites. Forums and YouTube help videos will guide you through the teething problems, and although this will take a significant amount of time to learn initially, once learned you will have new skills and the control to update and evolve your own site, and you will have saved money. Make sure you pick a relevant or memorable domain name, plan what you want on the site, and set about creating it. Remember to look at search engine optimization (SEO), and consider marketing tools such as creating a blog to ensure readers are engaged and the site is constantly creating new content. Become savvy with Google and how it, and other search engines, will raise your website to the top of the listings.

If this is too involved for you, there are many companies providing website-building and maintenance services, including options abroad in places such as India, which can prove to be much cheaper.

Social Media

So now you've built an amazing website with ever-growing content and all your best promotional material. What will you do with it? A website that no one knows about is useless so it's time to promote it.

The easiest way at the moment is to integrate it with any and all of the popular social media sites. Create a Facebook page, Twitter account, Google profile, LinkedIn profile, and anything else that you can think of. Connect them all together so you can post on one and the others automatically show the post too. Create buttons and prompts on your website so people can click through and connect in all manners, as well as promote your website through the social media.

But be warned that incessant self-promotion is quite boring for others so use social media as a tool to interact with the people you want to interact with and allow the promotion to be a behind-the-scenes by-product of that interaction.

Subscription Sites

There are also many websites that artists and companies use to advertise their music jobs. These can be a great way to discover musical opportunities, as well as creating your own profile so that others can find you.

Such examples include Musiciannetworkpro, Starnow, and Music-jobs.com. More sites emerge on a regular basis and some are more useful than others. Any free subscriptions are certainly worth doing, but many of these charge a fee so you will need to research how useful each site actually looks and whether you think the outlay is likely to offer a good return in paid work or experience.

Paid Advertising

There are advertising opportunities available to us at a reasonable cost on the Internet, Google Adwords and Facebook advertising being two of the main avenues to explore. These can be a very effective way to reach your targeted audience such as a South West London music teacher creating a Google advert that only shows when someone in South West London searches for "drum tutor." But beware that this can consume money quickly so if you feel that this might benefit you, test the water carefully, and keep your budget small.

Tell People

And don't forget to tell everyone you meet. Make sure the website is on your business cards so you can hand them out to everyone and pin them up on studio notice boards. Let the world know who you are, what you do, and where they can look you up.

SECRET 41: MAXIMIZE YOUR EMPLOYABILITY

Some drummers are lucky enough to get in a band with their friends after leaving school, write the music they love to play, and then enjoy a long, fruitful career playing this music. But they are a tiny percentage of all the drummers in the world. There are far more drummers who enjoy a living from drumming having worked incredibly hard and made compromises along the way. These compromises might include playing music they do not particularly love, dealing with unlikable employers/artists (no names mentioned!), and facing conditions that are not anywhere close to glamorous. But these drummers are making a living from their passion: drumming.

Even these drummers make up quite a small number relative to the number of drummers that exist. From the bedroom enthusiast to the weekend pub band performer, drummers are numerous, and if you want any chance of enjoying a sustainable career, then you need to maximize your employability.

The Drummer

First of all you should look at your drumming potential. If you are a rock drummer, then you can only find work in rock music situations. However, if you have studied and gained experience playing rock, funk, pop, metal, jazz, blues, Latin, and so on, then you will clearly have many more playing opportunities available to you as discussed in Secret 38.

Beyond styles, it is crucial that you read music to a great standard. Now you can do sessions, theater work, cruise ships, and a whole lot more that wouldn't have been available to a non-reader.

Can you play to a click? Great, a drummer who doesn't have that skill in today's music industry will not go far.

A great deal of music also uses technology now so as a drummer you must be familiar with triggers, samplers, drum machines, and backing tracks as discussed in Secret 30.

And if you have these skills, let people know about them. Get out there and talk to people; mention it on your website and social media profiles. Make sure the world knows what you can do.

Beyond Drumming

Unfortunately the truth is that many of us can't sustain a good income from drumming alone. It is therefore necessary to diversify and offer a range of other services that either help tide you over in quiet spells or that make you more employable than "just a drummer."

Programmer

Many tracks today use programmed drums, but someone still has to program these patterns. Learn the equipment, learn how to program the beats, and get out there to offer your services.

Producer

Many drummers are also very knowledgeable in the studio environment. This is helped by the accessibility to equipment and subsequent increased number of home studios allowing drummers to get hands-on experience right through the recording chain. Learn how to record other instruments as well and you can start offering your services as a producer.

Songwriter

If you have some basic skills on a second instrument, develop this and try your hand at composition. Artists often enjoy using a writing partner so you can offer your services in this area. It also means you can contribute more in band writing sessions and understand the language of the other musicians. The songwriter royalties should motivate as much as anything else.

Multi-Instrumentalist

As well as song writing, a second instrument can be a great asset to a band. If looking for a drummer who offers backing vocals then a band will pick you, the singing drummer, over the tone-deaf drummer. If you play congas, djembe, piano, fiddle, bagpipes, or anything else, get out there and let people know. Who knows when a musical director will be looking for a drummer who also plays a little bit of ukulele and bagpipes for the next major artist's world tour? And they'll think of you.

Be Different

There are so many drummers out there, and so many good ones. So how will you stand out from the rest? Try to find a niche. It might be to do with your appearance, your styles of music, your use of technology, you integration of art forms. Anything that you can do to separate yourself from the crowd and become memorable will aid you in your search for continuous employment. Consider all your skills and attributes and think of how you can market this effectively.

Teacher

Many drummers will also teach their craft alongside performing it. This is not for everyone and does require a great deal of patience, but if you are the right sort of person, then this can offer you a great steady income and a lot of reward when seeing your students progress. You can do this through an establishment or privately to keep control of the hours you work.

The key to any of these roles is to embrace them and not consider them as a chore that takes you away from drumming. You are still in a creative musical environment and not serving burgers or sitting in an office. And you are still mixing with music professionals so the networking is occurring for future opportunities, which is less likely to happen at a burger bar.

SECRET 42: KEEPING THE GIGS—BEYOND DRUMMING

So you've created your website, you've littered the social media world with your networking efforts, you've been to every jam night, you've taken every gig that comes your way, and now the world is starting to see that you're quite a good drummer.

But there is a lot more to being a successful drummer than just drumming. This idea of "who you know, not what you know" rings true and it is your whole reputation that will eventually make or break you as a career musician. Getting the gigs is one thing, but career longevity can require a degree of interpersonal skills and diplomacy.

If you consider a typical working day for a musician, the actual music part of it is relatively small; therefore the other aspects of day-to-day life are also very important. One of the main aspects is being a pleasure to be around. If there is any aspect of your personality that will upset people, it is likely to come out on a tour when you share the same company every hour of every day. Here are some points to consider that go beyond the music.

Turn Up Prepared

Never be the one that turns up to rehearsals unprepared. You will regret it instantly when singled out as the only person who hasn't done the homework. While people want to move through material and get out of that stuffy rehearsal room as quickly as possible, they will soon become short-tempered with the lazy drummer who didn't bother to put in preparation time.

Don't Whine

Things go wrong, schedules extend beyond their allotted time, hire kits aren't quite what you wanted, the hotel breakfast isn't what you would normally choose, you miss your wife, you realized you hate your wife and want a divorce . . . whatever is niggling you, make a conscious effort not to let the world know about it every five minutes. No one enjoys the company of a whiner. If it's a music-related problem, try to solve it quickly and quietly, and whatever the result is, try to carry out a professional job without letting the world know what a struggle it was.

Be Punctual

Don't be the last person down to the hotel lobby when everyone is there waiting for you. Be the first person to rehearsal to set up your drum kit so you're ready to play when everyone else turns up. Being punctual goes a long way, and it's easy to do by just leaving yourself enough time.

Be Friendly

This might be obvious, but it's very easy over time to allow your basic joviality to slip. You don't necessarily need to pretend to be someone you're not, but be aware that you are in a situation with other people who haven't necessarily chosen to be with each other and therefore making a little effort to be a considerate, friendly person can go a long way.

Diplomacy

To enforce that point further, this is a good exercise in diplomacy. If someone has a habit that drives you mad, don't bottle it up until you explode in a fit of rage. Take a deep breath, think calming thoughts, and find a way to politely ask them not to do something. Small niggles can become major aggravations in extended close-quarter living conditions so find ways to deal with things and keep the peace.

Be Hygienic

Let's be honest with ourselves, would you want to live on a tour bus with someone who performs a sweaty concert each night and only showers once a week? Keep yourself clean, keep your clothes clean, keep your sleeping area tidy, and pray that the rest of the group do the same.

Consider Others

Just thinking about your actions and the impact they have on others can really help. If you are listening to loud music in the early hours through your headphones and it's keeping the others awake in the bunk above you, they will soon grow tired of you.

Rein In Your Indulgences

If you're going on tour with Motörhead, you might find that heavy drinking is compulsory, but many professional musical situations will not tolerate such behavior. A touring lifestyle can take its toll on even the most balanced characters, so make sure that you don't slip into the common pitfalls. The biggest impact might be a detrimental effect on your ability to perform at the gig. But beyond that, a hungover wreck is not the best company.

CHAPTER 9

Recording Strategies

SECRET 43: PLAY LESS

Most drummers are guilty of overplaying at some point in their career, and it is usually the inexperienced drummers that exude this trait more frequently. As we learn new techniques and tricks, we feel desperate to show the world at every given opportunity, regardless of how this affects the music.

The result is that we sound egotistical, selfish, and completely unaware of our musical surroundings. Rather than the world elevating us to god-like status, listeners will most likely dismiss us as foolish and infantile.

Over time we learn this, and it's often learned the hard way when someone is paying for studio time and getting frustrated at what you're producing.

I run my own drum studio, which gives me the chance to try ideas out before sending them to the artist for whom I'm working. Generally my first take is too busy. I try things that seem like a great idea, but when I listen back, it sounds cluttered and unprofessional. I then strip the parts back and allow the song to breathe, resulting in a great-sounding drum part.

It is very rare that I listen back and think, "I wish I had played more." It's usually the opposite. And it's even rarer that a client has asked me to play more.

Another consideration is the fact that the drums are often recorded at the early stages. You might not have any idea of what will be added to the track further down the line. It could be congas, tambourine, shakers, brass instruments, and anything else. By trying to fill up all the space at this early stage, you might have ruined the ideas for additional parts later.

Next time you listen to the radio, really examine what the drums are doing. You will find that a great deal of mainstream music will consist of seemingly mundane drum parts that simply provide the appropriate rhythm to make the song groove. But these simple rhythms will be played with such precision and feel that the whole track will make you want to move somehow. That is the art of the studio drummer. And it is having a passion for finding that simple pattern and making it groove as much as possible, as well as finding that choice fill at the appropriate moment, that will help you succeed in this environment.

As an exercise, try recording yourself to a backing track of mainstream, radio-friendly music (this exercise isn't relevant for genres such as heavy metal or progressive rock where the drums are often granted more freedom). Perform two different drum recordings. One will be an all-out assault of technique and chops. The second will be as simple as you possibly can. Think total restraint. Minimize fills; don't feel obliged to alter the groove just because it hasn't been changed in four bars. Stick to the pattern and make it feel good.

Now change your metaphorical hat to that of the artist or producer. Listen back to each recording and really think about which one makes the song sound better. Ignore how excited you are by your own drum skills. Think about the song. Imagine which track you would most like to hear on the radio while singing along on a long car journey.

If you are considering this exercise seriously, you should opt for the simpler part. You may decide that it could benefit from another fill leading into the chorus, or other such small changes, but overall you should find it enhances the song more than the busy drum take. Enhancing the song is discussed more in the next secret.

SECRET 44: PLAYING FOR THE SONG

Playing for the song is a crucial aspect for any drummer, but especially a studio drummer who is committing his or her ideas to the eternal recorded format of choice.

A large part of this concerns the subject discussed in the last secret: overplaying. There we carried out the exercise to see whether a busy drum part enhanced the song more or less than a simple drum part.

And it is that phrase that should be at the forefront of your mind when creating a drum part: "enhancing the song." Every note you play should make the song sound better. We are not adding drums to a track for the sake of it; we are aiming to make it sound better, and every single note you play affects that song.

In essence, playing for the song is just a mindset. It is about having a sympathetic ear and taking on a musical approach rather than just a drummer's approach. You must listen to the song in the most musical way and think about the textures and layers of sound that you can provide to improve the song. One example is the 1970 Simon and Garfunkel track "Bridge Over Troubled Water," where legendary studio drummer Hal Blaine brought snow chains into the studio and dragged them along a cement floor, as well as slapping them down on the floor to create a certain sound effect that he envisaged in his mind. This is well outside the zone of normal drumming, but Blaine felt this particular sound would create the right soundscape to enhance the mood of the song.

So other than playing to a click with great timing, on great-sounding drums, here are some thoughts that you may wish to adopt in your next studio situation.

1. Focus on the whole song, not just the inner workings of the drummer. Consider the whole song and think about the parts you could use, the speed of the song (not just tempo but the way the music moves within each bar), the textures that you could provide.

2. Listen to the singer foremost. Listen to the phrasing, how the lyrics move. Think about the lyrical content. What mood is he or she creating?

3. Do everything for a reason. Don't go to the ride cymbal just because you're bored of playing the hi-hats. Go there because the song needs a lift or different timbre.

4. Think about your employer. Try to establish what each producer or artist is looking for. This can vary dramatically, and learning how to interpret people's (sometimes confusing) descriptions is part of the job. Once you get to know a person, this can become intuitive, but in the beginning you might have to work hard to read someone.

As an exercise, try playing to the same backing track that you used in Secret 43. Record yourself again but really focus on this aspect of playing for the song. Don't be afraid to think outside of the box. Let your imagination and emotions get deep inside the music and see what you come up with. It may be no different than before, or it might be completely different. Have a go and see what the result is.

SECRET 45: ACHIEVING A GREAT TONE

Inexperienced studio drummers will suffer from three main problems: playing inappropriately, playing inaccurately, and failing to create a good sound.

The timing issues were covered in the "Timing Strategies" section of this book, and playing appropriately was covered in the last secret. So all that remains is the drum sound.

A large part of this comes down to good drums, the right heads, and effective tuning, which were also discussed earlier in the book. But even with these factors taken care of, it is still possible for a human to make the drum sound bad.

It never ceases to amaze me as a teacher when I hear students come in to my studio and play on my kit. Every individual makes the exact same instrument sound different. Some have an innate ability to make the drums sing and sound beautiful; others make them sound like old plastic tubs.

Every recording engineer will tell you that the key to a great drum sound is to get a great drummer on a great drum kit in a great-sounding room. Then the microphones will pick up a great sound with ease. Many drummers think that they can get away with a lazy approach in the modern recording environment where so much seems possible in the control room with effects and editing software. This attitude is very unprofessional and will make sure you are never called for work again.

The first part is to make sure the drums actually sound good. I used to think my drums were OK, but then when I sound checked them, I always felt embarrassed because in that exposed environment, I knew each individual drum didn't sound great on its own. This is largely down to tuning so make sure that each drum sounds great individually when you strike it.

Where Are You Striking the Drum?

We are all taught from early on that a drum sounds best when hit in the middle, and this is correct. But it is not always the sound we want. Sometimes we may want a rim shot on the snare played close to the edge of the head to achieve a timbale sound or even on the toms for certain effects. But make sure it is the right sound. Take care to achieve exactly what you want to hear on the recording. Sometimes you may want a cross stick. Make sure you achieve that nice, full, woody tone by striking it in the right place.

But often the middle of the drum is where we will get the best tone. Be sure to strike it with appropriate force. If it is a big tom tuned low for rock, you might find that a certain amount of force is required to create a pleasing tone. You might have a higher tuning for a jazz track that sounds better when hit with less force. But power aside, the main culprit for diminished drum resonance is poor technique and failure to rebound. Read Secret 12 where this is discussed.

How Are You Hitting the Hi-hats?

With such an expressive voice of the kit, it is crucial to consider how you are using this sound. A shoulder of the stick on the edge of the hi-hat creates a very different sound to the tip of the stick playing halfway onto the hi-hat. Choose which is best for this part of the track. See how you can build the track by changing the sound of the hi-hats. Consider a varied pattern that might involve accents and non-accents. In time the correct sound will be found subconsciously, but until then, really think about the sound you want and how you can obtain that.

Consistency

Once you have the drums sounding great, and you are playing each part of the kit with the correct technique, volume, and timbre, you will hopefully find great pleasure in laying down a very simple groove. With the kit sounding so good, even the simplest of rhythms is enjoyable and effective. This should help you to stay disciplined and avoid overplaying.

But a key characteristic of great drummers is consistency. Every snare hit will be on the same part of the drumhead, with the same technique and same power. If you do not have that consistency, it will be a distraction on the record. One of the best ways to learn this consistency is to record yourself and listen back to each hit. If one snare note is louder, it will stand out and you will easily realize why this is not acceptable.

Remember, the drummers with a full diary are often required to play the simple rhythms for 90 percent of the time. But it is those drummers that execute the simple stuff with perfect feel, appropriate parts, great tone, and complete consistency who are called back time and time again.

SECRET 46: MIX YOURSELF

Having identified three main problems for studio drummers in the last secret, here we will focus on a subject that broadly falls under the category of two of them: playing inappropriately and failing to create a good sound.

Studio recording requires the ability to create great feel and energy while maintaining total control and discipline. An animalistic, frenzied assault of the drums that might be perfect for a festival gig will possibly be too chaotic and uncontrolled for the studio. And yet as drummers we still want the energy and vibe to come through on our recordings so they don't sound sterile and lifeless.

Achieving this is not easy, which is why many drummers fall down at this hurdle. One of the main problems drummers face is getting carried away and hitting things too hard. It is not necessary in the studio environment as we don't need to fight against screaming guitars to reach 20,000 people. The drums have microphones and the levels can be brought up to the required volume. In fact, the tone of the drum might be choked if you hit it too hard.

But even worse than hitting the drum too hard is the problem of too much volume on the cymbals. The high frequency sound that is created from cymbals bleeds into everything, whether it's a sloshing open hi-hat, big crash cymbal, or a monstrous ride cymbal. The sounds are long and very abrasive, and once they've bled into the snare microphone, there's only so much the producer or engineer can do to eradicate that sound and isolate the drum kit voice that the microphone was intended to record.

I discovered this the hard way when recording a rock album with heavy hi-hats. Many of the tracks involved an open hi-hat sound and I was playing with the same volume I used live. When it came to mixing we realized that the snare microphone contained so much hi-hat bleed that we couldn't bring the volume up very high before the hi-hat dominated everything. Gating and EQ could only do so much; therefore the power of the snare drum had to be sacrificed and the recording suffered. From this I learned to play the hi-hat less forcefully and also use lighter hi-hats in the studio.

Being aware of your whole sound is crucial in the studio and also a huge benefit live. Prolific studio drummers such as Steve Gadd had the ability to play with such great sound balance across their kit that engineers barely had to mix them as they were naturally mixing themselves as they played. If you make life easy for the guys in the control room, they are more likely to call you back next time.

To really gauge how you sound when you play, try recording yourself with a single microphone to get an idea of the balance of sound that you produce. Use a standard vocal dynamic microphone, such as a Shure SM58, just behind your ear when you sit at the drum stool. This way it will pick up exactly what you hear from the drum kit.

This will give you an idea of how balanced you sound. If all you can hear is cymbals, try again with less cymbal volume. Experiment until it sounds just right. But remember, the trick here is to alter certain volumes when required without losing the feel or intensity of your playing.

CHAPTER 10

Performance Strategies

SECRET 47: WARM-UP AND GIG PREPARATION

The physicality of drumming requires a fit and well-prepared body for optimal performance. This is crucial if we want to play at our best level, avoid injury, and continue to play the drums as part of a long and demanding career.

We have already discussed some of the risks in Secrets 31–34, and many of the prevention methods included warming up.

To start with, good cardiovascular fitness will enable you to better handle your job and feel more confident about achieving your goals. I know that when I'm in top form, I can't wait to get on stage and enjoy what I'm playing. On the other hand, when I'm feeling sluggish, I become more apprehensive.

Body Fuel

But even when in top form, we must prepare our muscles, tendons, and ligaments for the exertion and demands placed upon them when drumming. An athlete wouldn't prepare for a race with a cigarette and a pint of beer, and we drummers should adopt the same mindset.

As well as avoiding cigarettes and alcohol, the food we consume will have a massive impact on our energy and focus levels. This seems obvious when we participate in sports, but a gruelling two-hour gig will also take its toll on your body if you don't have the right fuel. The foods provided prior to a performance tend to be rich, fatty, and lacking in the nutrients we actually need. A bacon roll and bottle of beer will not do, even if a bowl of M&Ms with all the red ones removed is added to the menu! If this is what you're eating before a show, then sometime during it, you are likely to feel an energy crash; you might become distracted and experience tempo issues, catastrophizing (see Secret 48), and general loss of enjoyment.

Generally speaking, prepare healthy snacks to maintain energy levels before you arrive at the venue and avoid the huge pre-gig dinner, which can leave you bloated and lethargic. Moreover, under the glare of lights or in an overheated venue, dehydration is another risk, so make sure you are drinking steadily. Always have a bottle of water beside you for easy regular intake, and make sure that there is plenty on stage for the performance.

Warm Up

Returning to the sporting analogy, it seems obvious that one shouldn't run, say, a 100-meter sprint with cold muscles. And yet so many drummers will go flying into an energetic gig without preparing their muscles for it. This is one of the surest ways of increasing your risk for injury. You will also find that you take the first two or three songs to warm up and actually reach your best playing level. Relatively easy fills might feel less achievable and your arm muscles may feel stiff. As well as injury, this increases the potential for poor performance and anxiety.

Warming up is really just a matter of getting the blood pumping through the muscles and making sure they can ease into the activity rather than being thrown into it without warning.

Many drummers find that a simple combination of rudiments is enough. You could try playing single strokes, double strokes, paradiddles, and anything else. Start slowly and softly and as you naturally warm into it you can increase the speed and intensity. To prepare yourself for playing, you may wish to try certain intricate patterns or anything specific to that particular show to reassure yourself that you are ready for the task in hand. It is also wise to carry out similar foot exercises to make sure your legs are ready for drumming. This can be done on the floor or via a bass pedal and bass drum practice pad such as the Pearl BD-10 or DW's Steve Smith bass drum practice pad.

As the old adage goes, "Fail to prepare and you prepare to fail," so take heed.

SECRET 48: STAGE FRIGHT

Most drummers have experienced nerves in some capacity before a gig, audition, or recording session. It may occur just before the performance or days in advance and manifest itself as a nervous anticipation that stimulates an inspired performance or a debilitating dread that actually prevents you going on stage.

Drugs are a common answer to anxiety and insecurity, but smoking increases the heart rate and therefore stress levels, alcohol impairs performance, and illegal substances become a crutch and then an addiction and ultimately destroy lives. Another common choice is the use of beta blockers, but this results in drummers resigned to just surviving a performance and losing all feel and connection to the music. Finally we have the problem of this being a slightly taboo subject, with musicians often keeping quiet through fear of appearing unprofessional or inferior.

Do I Have Stage Fright?

We must distinguish between stage fright and the more serious music performance anxiety (MPA). Stage fright affects around 80 percent of drummers, causing symptoms such as the psychological self-doubt or expectation of failure, as well as the physical sweaty palms, muscle tension, palpitations, short breath, dry mouth, and shaking hands.

Common stage fright often stimulates arousal, which allows a positive, energetic performance. If our state of arousal is too low when we drum, the performance will be lackluster. But it is when this nervous reaction becomes debilitating that we have a problem.

This is when a drummer is suffering from MPA: an experience of persisting anxiety or even physical changes that hamper a performance, regardless of ability and experience.

MPA might manifest itself as anxiety, panic, memory loss, poor concentration, unusual breathing, sweating, increased heart rate, dry mouth, trembling, technical errors, difficulty moving naturally, or even avoiding performing.

Dr. Louise Montello comments,[1] "I see the sense of dread replace the original joy of music making. This can make playing music more of a chore than something that exhilarates and heals. The worst case scenario is that the stage fright is so severe that drummers have difficulty maintaining a steady beat, possibly leading to performance mastery issues or giving up their career. I also see how the stress associated with stage fright can create unhealthy movement patterns that can lead to injuries in drummers."

Causes

Montello says, "Serious performance anxiety can be traced to unresolved past traumas around performing and/or other issues like abuse, accidents, loss, etc."

Sean Grey, emotional freedom technique expert, adds,[2] "When an artist is about to perform, often their biggest challenge is dealing with the emotional pressure of the occasion. The fear of failure, being judged, or letting themselves and others down."

Certainly fixating on the audiences' evaluation of your performance is a common issue. This critical evaluation could be deemed to be coming from total strangers, or close friends. In fact 10,000 strangers might be less daunting than a crowd of just five drummers.

Many drummers are noted for their perfectionism. This might be the motivation behind many great performances, but it can also lead to misery. They feel that their self-worth as a drummer is reliant on each performance being impeccable. Often these sufferers won't accept praise from others, and so every performance is destined to appear as a failure.

The constant struggle with perfectionism and self-worth is sometimes accompanied by "catastrophizing": obsessing about negative events that will most likely not happen. These could include dropping a drumstick, falling off your stool, missing a cymbal, or forgetting your parts. Subsequently, we may become overly aware of the physical changes caused by the anxiety. What starts as slightly sweaty palms or fast breathing is seen as a sign of forthcoming disaster, and huge anxiety is created out of nothing.

Although MPA is only found from adolescence upward, and more frequently in females, it can seem indiscriminate by disregarding skill and experience. Ironically it's found in the higher-level drummers quite frequently. Having performed at a very high level, the drummer is conditioned to think that every performance must meet these self-imposed standards, and therefore anxiety is attached to every performance.

Learn to Love Drumming Again

Here is a three-part strategy to help overcome self-doubt and anxiety.

1. Pre-gig warm-up

This important aspect was discussed in depth in Secret 47, so ensure you schedule time for rudimental pad work, stretches, or whatever works for you so your body is ready to get up and perform from the first note to the last. While warming up, try to instill positive thoughts in your mind. Don't focus on the nonexistent

overcritical audience. Instead visualize a positive response. Imagine yourself playing at your best level and enjoying the experience.

2. Equipment, preparation, and during the gig

Be prepared and capable and you will have nothing to fear. Choose repertoire
that is well within your ability where possible. If you are forced to play something
challenging, practice until it's comfortable. The greater the challenge, the greater
your risk of MPA. Before an audition, gather as much information on what the
band or artist wants as you can. Learn their material inside out, get there early, and
make sure you have the right equipment to be at ease.

Be sure to pace yourself at gigs. Think about the length of your set. A
10,000-meter runner wouldn't start as quickly as a 100-meter sprinter. If he did
he would soon fatigue. You can also fatigue too early, which means you won't be
able to keep time, your coordination will become sloppy, and your technique will
diminish. That doesn't mean you should be lackluster for the first few songs, but
learn how to create energy in your playing without using unnecessary effort. This
might mean developing better technique, setting your kit up more ergonomically,
or playing with less tension.

It might also come down to breathing. Many drummers do forget to breathe
when concentrating too hard or playing difficult parts. This is denying our body
of the thing it needs most: oxygen. Without it, our muscles are deprived of their
fuel and the heart works faster. We are trying to avoid stress so increasing heart
rates and overworking muscles are counterproductive. This was discussed in depth
in Secret 7.

It's also important to control the situation as much as possible. Make sure you
have the best equipment available to you. Take time to tune your drums so they
sound great. Make sure you get the correct mix in your monitors at sound check.
If your drums sound great, then you will feel confident and inspired.

3. More serious sufferers

Continuously debating who the best drummer in the world is, and such competi-
tions as the World's Fastest Drummer, may serve a purpose in music, but they also
have the potential to misguide us. Music is not a competition; it differs from sport
in this way. Music is an art form. There is no "best drummer in the world"; there
are only individual opinions. All drummers have the ability to move their listeners, whether they've played drums for a month or a decade. If the rhythm plays
a part in creating an emotion in their listeners, then it has achieved the greatest
thing that music can.

My experience is that the drumming community is a very warm, supportive, and welcoming group that love sharing their passion and encouraging one another. Art is subjective; play with passion, commit to each note, and lose yourself in the music. As drummers we should not focus on a judgmental audience, but on the joy of being on stage making music.

However, if we experience serious MPA, it may take more specialized approaches. A good starting point would be associations such as BAPAM (British Association for Performing Arts Medicine) which exist to help musicians with all health issues for free or little cost. This might involve seeing an expert like Dr. Carol Chapman, who offers therapies such as cognitive behavioral therapy and personal construct psychotherapy.

Alternatively Sean Grey suggests, "EFT and other energy therapies are able to deal with the fight or flight response to stress by balancing the body's energy system and reprogramming the subconscious that runs our life. It can also release the physical tension drummers experience from playing when their muscles are tight and tense. It can be used subtly before a performance and as tapping sends calming messages to the brain, the need for drugs, alcohol or smoking can be lessened. Once the negative belief has been cleared, positive affirmations can take hold."

These techniques may sound a little clinical or new age, but this is a psychological problem and a complex issue to tackle. When asked if we can completely get over MPA, Dr. Montello says, "Yes, through utilizing the Performance Wellness techniques (proper breathing, meditation, restructuring negative thoughts, connecting with your Essential Musical Intelligence) in daily life, performers can regain the joy of playing music and completely transform the victim stance into a deep, grounded sense of personal power and mastery."

It is important to remember that people want you to succeed. They go to watch a musical performance for enjoyment and want you to do well. The examiners want you to pass. People are there to support you, so why not support yourself?

If you are suffering from performance anxiety, it is important to seek suitable help. Explore the different options laid out here, get the right help, and get back to enjoying drumming the way you did when you first picked up a pair of sticks.

SECRET 49: BELIEVE IN YOURSELF

When teaching drum kit, it's astounding how uninspiring and boring a student can make a simple beat sound, and yet how great the next student can make the same beat sound. There are many factors that might affect this such as the nuances of their timing, where they strike the drum, the relative volume between their kit voices, and so on. But often it just comes down to self-belief.

If student A is a timid and shy person who struggles to perform to an audience even when it's just his or her teacher, this inner fear will often be highly audible in the sound he or she produces. The hesitant, tentative notes will lack the tone, clarity, and power that are required for the rhythm to move its listener.

If student B, full of confidence and self-belief, then plays the beat, it is suddenly brought to life, inspiring the listeners to play their instruments along, tap their feet, move their heads, or dance. It has achieved all that a drum rhythm should achieve.

Of course, it isn't always as simple as that, and this example only really serves to illustrate a point. And while too much confidence isn't always a good thing, it is often the case that trepidation and fear are very inhibitive when performing.

However, drummers are also human beings, and it is unrealistic to assume that all drummers should be free from self-doubt and too simplistic to suggest that they should just "get over it." And if stage fright or musical performance anxiety is an issue, read Secret 48.

But it is certainly worth really thinking about your playing and trying to establish if every note of every performance is as good as it could be. Years ago I saw Kenny Aronoff perform and was struck by his force behind the drums. He didn't necessarily play anything technically awe inspiring (although everything he played was perfect for each song); it was simply that he played every note with total conviction. That night I really felt his sincerity and responded to the way he put his whole self into the performance.

That performance forced me to reassess myself and ascertain whether I put the same energy into every note that I play. Aronoff had played even the simplest beats with such self-belief that this carried through into me, the listener, so that I bought into his grooves as well. It was as if his self-belief was transported through his rhythms into me and I believed in those rhythms, which made them so much more effective and powerful.

It's not a simple case of hitting the drums harder and louder. This was not necessarily about volume, but about meaning every note. Each note was intended and existed to enhance the music. As well as believing in yourself and the notes that you are playing, part of this comes down to playing everything for a reason, not just adding notes for the sake of it.

So treat every performance like your last, play each note with total conviction, and make sure that every note counts.

Of course, if you are well prepared for a performance, it is so much easier to actually be confident about what you're playing. But even if you are thrown in as a last-minute dep, it can be a state of mind that helps you succeed. Tell yourself that you are capable; persuade yourself that this is a great, enjoyable experience that you should cherish; and give the performance everything you've got.

If you have any recording of yourself that you are not happy with, try re-recording yourself with a renewed sense of self-belief and conviction. Hopefully your state of mind will be clear for all to hear on the recording.

NOTES

1. Dr. Montello, e-mail interview with author on September 20, 2012.
2. Sean Grey, e-mail to author on September 23, 2012.

CHAPTER 11

Soloing Strategies

SECRET 50: SOLOING WITH A THEME

There are mixed opinions among drummers respecting the drum solo. Some of us crave the thirty-minute extravaganza in the tradition of rock giants like John Bonham or Joey Jordison, letting the spotlight shine on the often overlooked rhythm maker. Others are repulsed by this needless self-indulgence during a concert when musicality seems to fall by the wayside to make room for a cacophony of noise and stick-wielding athletics.

But if we take a closer look at some of the great musical soloists, such as be-bop great Max Roach, we can see carefully thought-out thematic and structural ideas that form the bases of the drum solo.

Love them or hate them, as drummers we are likely to be faced with the request for a drum solo at least once in our careers, and if performed without any prior thought, these can loom as a potentially scary, unwieldy mess of notes. However, if you are physically and mentally prepared beforehand, these can become a joyous springboard for musical freedom and self-expression. One approach is to incorporate a large element of improvisation within a set of structural or thematic confines, as outlined below.

Consider Max Roach again, who many acknowledge as a highly melodic drummer who also thought in terms of form and structure. Take as an example the song "Delilah" from the *Clifford Brown and Max Roach* recording in 1954. There we can distinctly hear Roach playing within the confines of the classic AABA 32-bar jazz form.

Throughout much of the solo the hi-hats on two and four are maintained to ground the whole solo, while his phrasing elsewhere often takes him across beats and over the bar lines. Instead of moving quickly from idea to idea, Roach develops each idea, making great use of repetition. His ideas can be clearly heard in sections, lasting four bars each before moving on to the next subdivision or phrasing. Rather than lashing out randomly at the drums, each phrase is intentional: he means every note, and every note counts. Furthermore, paraphrasing allows Roach to bring back ideas from earlier in the solo, which also gives the listener the chance to recognize patterns and experience a journey rather than an onslaught of noise.

So here we have a clearly thought-out and structured musical performance, rather than a panicked attack of the drums, with the drummer trying to play as quickly as possible for the sake of speed.

Exercise 1

As an exercise, create a theme. It should be a small rhythmic idea that could also have a melody attached, one that can be sung in your head as you solo.

You could use whatever suits your needs, but I will use "Blue Monk" by Thelonious Monk to illustrate a point. Here is the melody rhythm written on the snare drum with the hi-hat pedaled on beats two and four.

Figure 11.1.

First practice it by playing the melody rhythm exactly as written on the snare with two and four on the hi-hat.

Exercise 2

Once you feel comfortable with this, you can begin to get creative with your orchestration. Move that melody around the kit, either with planned or improvised voicing. Below is an example.

Figure 11.2.

Exercise 3

The next step is to embellish the melody. This could involve playing notes in the spaces around the melody, as well as actually altering the melody rhythm itself. Below is an example based upon Exercise 2, with both options for embellishment included.

Figure 11.3.

Exercise 4

By this stage you should feel quite comfortable with the melody themes and can begin to get creative while maintaining the melody in your mind. Start to venture away from the melody rhythm, improvising by feel but always with the melody rhythm in mind. This way you will naturally carve an improvisation around that rhythmic theme, able at any point to return to the theme. Even when improvising away from the theme, it will still be implied, providing the underlying structure that will bring order and musical sense to your solo.

These exercises will not apply to all situations, but you can certainly practice them within the contexts of various genres, serving as a foundation for when that band leader turns around on stage to face you and spontaneously shouts, "Drum solo!"

SECRET 51: ODD NUMBERED GROUPINGS

One of the first fills we learn is groups of four sixteenth notes moving round each drum. When soloing, many experienced drummers still resort to this safe ground because it is so easy and natural. Of course this phrasing is effective. But in your search for more interesting phrases around the kit, start by looking at odd numbers.

Here we will examine three-, five-, and seven-note phrases. You can play these in any time signature and over any subdivision, but we will begin in common time over sixteenth notes. These examples focus on simple orchestrations, but once you become familiar with the phrases, you will be able to move freely across the drum kit and create some exciting patterns.

Although our convenient sixteenth note phrases fit neatly into common time, when dealing with odd numbered phrases we have to work out the mathematics because sixteen is not divisible by three, five, or seven.

Therefore, for each phrase, I have included a single bar with any required additional notes to fit into the single bar, as well as an example of several bars until that phrase naturally resolves.

Exercise 1

Here we are looking at three-note phrases. Three goes into sixteen five times with one remaining. Try playing this as a single bar fill in sequence with a bar of eight beats. The right hand is written on the high tom while the left hand plays the snare drum.

Figure 11.4.

Exercise 2

And now we have the three-note phrase over the three bars that it takes to resolve.

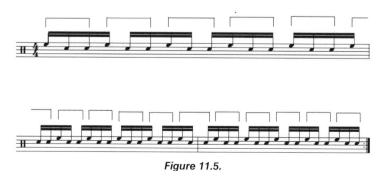

Figure 11.5.

Exercise 3

Now we are looking at five-note phrases. This phrase goes into a bar three times with one note remaining. The left hand stays on the snare drum while the right hand moves down the toms for each new phrase. Again, try it in a sequence with a rock beat.

Figure 11.6.

Exercise 4

This five-note phrase takes five bars to resolve.

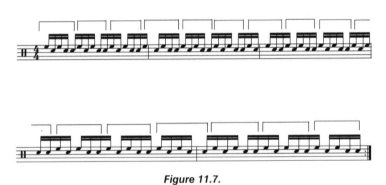

Figure 11.7.

Exercise 5

The seven-note phrase goes into the sixteenth notes twice with two extra notes at the end (played here on the floor tom). This works well as a fill in its own right.

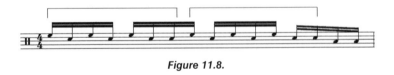

Figure 11.8.

Exercise 6

And then here we see the seven phrase played over sixteenth notes. This takes a full seven bars to resolve. It could be used in its entirety, or in part only, before moving to something else. The left hand remains on the snare while the right hand moves from high tom, through medium tom, to low tom, and then back again.

Figure 11.9.

Once you have become comfortable with each phrasing, consider different or-chestrations around the kit. Think how you can bring these ideas into a creative and musical solo. Consider different phrases beyond three, five, and seven. Also consider bringing different phrases together in a sequence. Remember also to look beyond sixteenth notes and use these ideas over various subdivisions and time signatures and also in a swung context.

SECRET 52: JUMPING INTO THE ABYSS—IMPROVISING

Some drummers love improvising more than anything else; others fear it above all else. But love it or hate it, it is a crucial aspect for being a great drummer. Often music is not planned, and you will have to play spontaneously. Sometimes you will be asked to solo in these situations, and you need to be ready for that.

But the funny thing about improvising is that you've just got to do it. Amid all the advice and strategies to develop your skills at improvisation, the most important thing you can do is to just do it.

So much of the success at improvisation comes down to confidence. When we place certain pressures upon ourselves, they cause huge problems. One self-imposed fear is that we'll go wrong or run out of ideas. Another is that you won't impress people sufficiently.

Dealing with that last fear, it is important not to consider your solo as something that needs to amaze everybody and take the spot as the greatest drum solo of all time. Don't try competing with Thomas Lang, Benny Greb, or anyone else. Be yourself and express your feelings in that moment through your instrument. Don't think of it as something that is being judged, but something spontaneous and creative that people will enjoy listening to.

As for the first fear, there is actually very little chance of going wrong or running out of ideas as long as you have practiced improvising to begin with. All you really need to do is stay in time. Anything else that happens within the music will sound fine because nobody knows what your intention was. If you make a mistake, don't cringe—just keep playing and the audience will be none the wiser.

Here are some tips and exercises to get you improvising and help develop that skill. As you do it more, your confidence will naturally grow. You will enjoy the chance to express yourself on your instrument and your solos will become musical and engaging.

Tips

What mood should you create? Think about the mood. If it is a dark and moody track, you might want the soft mallets on the toms. Could you use brushes? Could you use your hands and snare strainer off? Think musically rather than technically.

Take the listener on a journey. The most boring solos are those when the drummer starts playing as many notes as possible and continues until the end. Start quietly and sparsely before developing to your crescendo; start with hands and move to sticks; begin with snare turned off and develop until you turn it on; begin on just toms then work the other drums in; start with a foot ostinato and gradually introduce the hands; start with quarter notes and develop to thirty-second notes. Allow the solo to move in some way.

Don't think too hard. Thinking gets in the way of creative ideas. Shut the world out and let the music flow. My best and most creative drumming comes when I'm at home just pleasing myself. Trying to capture that on a stage is often the Holy Grail, and the more you can let yourself go on the stage, the more naturally your playing will flow.

Be Aware of the Sound You Are Producing

These exercises develop awareness of the notes you are playing, causing you to consider them rather than wildly thrashing at the drums.

Exercise 1

Improvise a bar and then immediately repeat it. Then without a pause play another bar and immediately repeat that. Continue with this theme. This constant flow of drumming doesn't give you much time to think about what you just played when repeating that bar so keep the ideas simple to begin with. Once you are comfortable, try playing two-bar phrases and repeating those.

Exercise 2

Pick a note value and stick to that. See how you can develop a single note value using different sounds and dynamics. Then pick a different note value and stretch that as far as you can.

Exercise 3

Pick one sound source and see what you can do with that. Develop the snare drum or a tom or the hi-hat as far as you can using rudiments, dynamics, and different sounds from that one source (see Secret 10).

Record Yourself

Exercise 1

Play a groove and then allow yourself a four-bar solo before bringing the groove back. Listen to the recording and consider it with an objective ear. What did you like? What didn't you like?

Exercise 2

As mentioned, often drummers race into the solo and don't allow it to develop. Even over a short four-bar period, you can develop the solo. But if you start blazing in at high volume with your fastest notes, the solo will be difficult to develop. Try recording a four-bar solo again and see how much you can evolve it.

Exercise 3

Once you've evolved the four-bar solo into something agreeable, extend the solo period and repeat the exercise. Always listen to the recording and evaluate.

Use a Theme

I like to start an improvised solo with a very basic theme in mind. I might begin by playing the theme before allowing the solo to evolve. But it often comes back around, or at least alludes to that theme throughout the solo.

Here are some ideas to use as your starting thematic idea:

1. a foot ostinato,
2. a rudiment,
3. a melody (see Secret 50),
4. a rhythm such as the Son Clave, or
5. a melodic phrase around the toms.

Use these exercises to help craft your ideas, but as mentioned, the most important thing is just to practice improvising, build your confidence, and learn how to develop your ideas.

BOOKS

Bailey, Colin. *Bass Drum Control.* Milwaukee, WI: Hal Leonard, July 1998.

———. *Bass Drum Control Solos.* Milwaukee, WI: Hal Leonard, August 2002.

Collins English Dictionary (third edition). Glasgow, Scotland: HarperCollins Publishers, 1991.

Culf, Nicola. *Musician's Injuries: A Guide to their Understanding and Prevention.* Kent, UK: Parapress, January 1998.

Gelb, Michael J. *Body Learning: An Introduction to the Alexander Technique.* New York: Henry Holt and Company, January 1996.

Harrison, Christine. *The Athletic Musician: A Guide to Playing Without Pain.* Lanham, MD: Scarecrow Press, February 1999.

Horvath, Janet. *Playing (Less) Hurt: An Injury Prevention Guide for Musicians.* Milwaukee, WI: Hal Leonard, May 2010.

Kabat-Zinn, Jon, and Andrew Weil. *Meditation for Optimum Health: How to Use Mindfulness and Breathing to Heal Your Body and Refresh Your Mind.* Louisville, CO: Sounds True, Incorporated, May 2001.

Norris, Richard. *The Musician's Survival Manual.* St. Louis, MO: MMB Music, August 1993.

WEBSITES

"About Tinnitus." American Tinnitus Association. www.ata.org/for-patients/about-tinnitus. Accessed May 27, 2013.

ONLINE VIDEO

"Dream Theatre Mike Mangini—Complete Interview." YouTube, 1:01, posted by "ArtisanNewsService." www.youtube.com/watch?v=SpazIte40rg. Accessed May 27, 2013.

DVDS

Bailey, Colin. *Bass Drum Technique*. 2011.
Caplan, Deborah, and Jane Kosminsky. *The Alexander Technique*. 2000.
Marsalis, Branford. *A Love Supreme*. 2004.

SONGS

Balkna Horses Band. "Kalajdzisko Oro." 2006.
Brown, Clifford, and Max Roach. "Delilah." 1954.
Brubeck, Dave. "Take Five." 1959.
Cahn, Sammy, and Jimmy Van Heusen. "Come Fly with Me." 1957.
Garfunkel, Art, and Paul Simon. "Bridge Over Troubled Water." 1970.
Jones, Ricky Lee. "Chuck E's in Love." 1979.
Led Zeppelin. "When the Levee Breaks." 1971.
Monk, Thelonious. "Blue Monk." 1954.
Radiohead. "15 Step." 2007.
Simon, Paul. "Oh, Marion." 1980.
Sting. "Seven Days." 1993.

"15 Step," 50

Ahead, 66
Akai, 84
Alesis, 84
Alexander Technique, 94, 96
Aronoff, Kenny, 141
The Athletic Musician: A Guide to Playing without Pain, 96

Baliey, Colin, 32
Balkan Horses Band, 50
BAPAM (British Association for Performing Arts Medicine), 140
Barrett, Carlton, 78
Bass Drum
    Techniques, 31–35
Beauford, Carter, 16
Blaine, Hal, 129
Blue Monk, 144
Body Learning: An Introduction to the Alexander Technique, 96
Bonham, John, 15, 36, 143
Bozzio, Terry, 18
Brazil, Karl, 82–84
Breathing, 12, 21
"Bridge Over Troubled Water," 129
Brown, Clifford, 143
Brubeck, Dave, 50
Bruford, Bill, 16, 99

Chapman, Dr. Carol, 140
"Chuck E's in Love," 15
Cobham, Billy, 99
Colaiuta, Vinnie, 28
Colato, Joe, 65
Collins, Phil, 12
"Come Fly with Me," 105
Cubase, 6, 85

DAW, 6, 40, 43, 82, 85
Dawson, Alan, 3
Davis, Miles, 15
Delilah, 143
Dream Theatre, 110, 111
Drumdial, 73
DW (Drum Workshop), 61, 136
Dynamics, 8

Ear plugs, 87–90
Emotional Freedom Technique (EFT), 138
Evans, 67, 74, 80

Feldenkrais Method, 94

Gadd, Steve, 15, 28, 60, 133
Garibaldi, David, 77
Greb, Benny, 150
Gretsch, 59
Grey, Sean, 140
Grip, 8, 26, 28–30

Jameson, Timothy, 91, 97, 98
Jones, Elvin, 49, 59
Jones, Rickie-Lee, 15
Jordison, Joey, 18, 59, 66, 143

Korg, 84

Lang, Thomas, 18, 150
Led Zeppelin, 15, 36
Logic Pro, 6, 85
A Love Supreme, 78
Ludwig, 77

Mangini, Mike, 110
Marley, Bob, 78
Marsalis, Branford, 78
McBrain, Nicko, 18
*Meditation for Optimum Health: How to
    Use Mindfulness and Breathing to
    Heal Your Body and Refresh Your
    Mind*, 94
Metallica, 66
Metronome, 8, 11, 15, 39–43, 54, 56, 81,
    85
MIDI, 6
Monk, Thelonious, 144
Montello, Dr. Louise, 137, 140
Moongel, 72, 73, 81
*Musician's Injuries: A Guide to their
    Understanding and Prevention*, 96
The Musician's Survival Manual, 96

Nakers, 28

"Oh Marion," 15

Palmer, Earl, 47
Pearl, 60, 61, 136
Pipe and tabor, 28
*Playing (Less) Hurt: An Injury Prevention
    Guide for Musicians*, 96
Portnoy, 111
Pro Tools, 85

Quarrier, Nicholas, 97

Radiohead, 50
Recording, 6, 10
Regal Tip, 65
Remo, 67, 68, 77, 78
Rich, Buddy, 19, 28
Roach, Max, 49, 143
Roland, 82–84
Rudiments 4, 13
    Double stroke roll 15, 26
    Flam, 8, 11, 53
    Paradiddle, 26
    Single stroke roll, 13, 22, 26, 27
Rudimental Ritual, 3, 4

"Seven Days," 50
Simon, Paul, 15
Simon and Garfunkel, 129
Sinatra, Frank, 105
Slipknot, 66
Smith, Steve, 136
Soloing, 18, 19
Sonor, 78
Sticking, 7–9, 13, 14
Sting, 50
Swinging, 47–49

Take That, 82
Tama, 60, 74
Technique, 21
Time Signatures, 50–52
Timing, 6, 8
Tinnitus, 87–89
Tower of Power, 77

Ulrich, Lars, 66

Watts, Jeff "Tain," 78
Weckl, Dave, 28
"When the Levee Breaks," 36
Williams, Robbie, 82
Williams, Tony, 15, 49

Yamaha, 59–61, 83, 84

Zildjian, 64, 89

About the Author

Matt Dean is a professional drummer, tutor, and author. Since achieving a First-Class BA (Hons) in contemporary music in 2003, he has worked as a freelance drummer playing most styles and situations live, in studios, and on TV. He runs a drum studio facility where he records drum tracks for artists around the world.

He has taught hundreds of drum students privately and in large groups, as well as giving workshops and clinics across the UK. He also set up and wrote the syllabus for the drumming division of the www.BecomeAMusicTeacher.com education company.

He has had feature articles published around the world in such music publications as *Modern Drummer* (U.S.), *Rhythm* (UK), *Drumscene* (Australia), *Making Music* (U.S.), *Music Teacher* (UK), and many more. He also publishes a drum blog through his website, www.mattdeanworld.co.uk, and has a book published by Scarecrow Press titled *The Drum: A History.*